House Guests and Ghosts:

Very True Stories of the Paranormal

By: Susan Mariani

TABLE OF CONTENTS

Foreword

What began as a short story about 'a day in the life' has developed a life of its own. As soon as I realized my son's imaginary friend perhaps wasn't imaginary and had affected many other family members and friends, I began asking questions; several of them offered information that was intriguing and quite frightening. As events were relayed to me throughout the years, I realized a pattern began to emerge and certain events couldn't be omitted or the reader would not fully understand what transpired. It was after our family reunion in St. Petersburg, Florida in nineteen eighty-three that I saw a family connection with the spiritual world that I didn't want to ignore.

We were often told as children that "the family that prays together stays together." We all would consider ourselves 'spiritual' but we are not all belonging to one denomination. My immediate family of ten siblings, all of my mother and father's siblings and their parents are devout Catholics. Growing up we prayed together every day as a family. In turn, we pray every day with our children. We often pray for the repose of the souls of 'the faithfully departed'. Although many of our cousins are scattered across the United States and even the globe, we get together every two to three years for a family reunion. We have been having our family reunions without interruption since nineteen eighty.

My grandparents got their children together for the first Genevie family reunion in 1967 at Cook's Forest State Park in Pennsylvania.

Every story in this book is true. There are skeptics among readers, just as there were among those who heard these tales first hand. If you pray, however, you believe in a spiritual realm co-existing with our own.

You believe in ghosts.

All stories have been told in the first person, those unable to be located or those requesting anonymity have been given false names. Every event involved a member of our family; either an immediate sibling or close relative. They all involved ghosts.

The ghosts in each incident appeared differently to each family member, too. Some were seen as though they were human, others as 'wisps' or orbs, still others as no more than a cold chill or shadow. In every case, the people who relayed these stories were absolutely certain that they were experiencing a paranormal event.

I've had the pleasure of meeting numerous WWII veterans as a member of the US LST Association and WWII Ranger Association; many told me horrific stories of combat and gallant tales of courage. Some relate these memories rather effortlessly, while others tend to relive the moment, becoming visibly upset and/or agitated. This is also true of those who came forward in this book. Certain traumatic events cause excessive emotion, and those who related supernatural phenomenon to me displayed the same type of emotion as the combat veterans.

I have researched all cases, looking at both scientific and medical explanations for each event, consulting experts when necessary. I've spent an enormous amount of time trying to ascertain why this particular family was chosen, the history behind the sightings, and any possible religious significance. I consulted a Catholic priest who is knowledgeable about the paranormal and exorcisms. He told me that he's never come across a family that has had so many paranormal experiences, but perhaps ours was chosen because they knew we'd help them 'find their way' through our prayers. He has asked that I not divulge his name, which I will honor.

I've read a multitude of books on ghosts and the paranormal, most suggest that the recipient of sightings are 'open' to it. I've found quite the opposite to be true. While the common denominator in these particular cases have been that all believe in God and are all related biologically, some more religious than others, not one wanted to see what they saw or experienced. Age was not a factor, either. The ghosts appeared to both the young and old, cynics, skeptics and believers; one going so far as to say after seeing the same ghost of a woman twice that he was "starting to" believe in ghosts. I have also read that people with diminished mental capacity are more vulnerable to spiritual encounters; my autistic son has had several. My dear cousin Katherine suffered with epilepsy her entire life, and was mildly diminished mentally because of her seizure disorder. She seemed to be more in touch with the unseen among us while she walked the Earth. She passed in 2002 and is missed immensely.

She visited her sisters shortly after her death as they were clearing out her room, greeting them as a burst of wind; sudden, forceful and chilling in her upstairs bedroom- with one window opened just slightly for ventilation. Her sisters were discussing how much "junk" she had accumulated at the time. They realized that their sister was unhappy with their comments, and apologized to her in audible voices! They both knew that burst of cold air was their sister, even though there is no scientific way to know. As of this publication, she has been resting in peace.

My prayer is that she, and all deceased members of our family, rest in eternal peace.

I want to thank everyone for entrusting me to relate their stories; taking time out of their hectic lives to assist in the research of their particular case.

This book is dedicated to my mother, Mary Jane (Genevie) Mariani, who by her life displayed love, courage, wisdom and compassion, teaching us that "we" are not in control here.

It is also dedicated to my eldest son, Vince, who lived through these traumatic events at a very tender age. Much of this story was told by one of the main characters through Vince; a ghost named Bacon. Vincent described his encounters with Bacon quite vividly with incredible recollection and detail, a large part of why I began to write these pages in the first place. He is my joy and inspiration, and one of the most courageous people I've ever met. I am very proud of him.

I am also sorry that I doubted you, Vince.

I would like to salute and thank the courageous men of the United States LST (Landing Ship Tank) Association, in particular ship #399 from the United States Navy. My uncle, Lou Genevie, served on that ship in the Pacific Theater during WWII, alongside my dear friend William (Bunker Bill) Jayne, Al DiMico, Joe DeMarco and Master Chief Joseph Earhart Sardo to name just a few.

I would also like to thank and salute the WWII Army Rangers for their many stories. All of our nation's veterans are remembered in our family's daily prayers.

My deepest thanks to my family-both immediate and extended- for tolerating my unending, probing questions. I love you all dearly and look forward to our next family reunion.

The e-mails contained in this book are in bold type. They have not been modified, corrected (grammar and spelling) or altered in any way. For security purposes, I have deleted last names and email addresses.

Chapter One

GETTING STARTED

Vincent was a moppy-haired, freckle-faced four year old when I took occupancy of the center apartment on Burton Avenue in Akron, Ohio. I'd rented the basement apartment from my eldest brother, David, when Vince was about 6 months old. After Dave was transferred out of town for business, I moved into the first floor. David owned the house, having purchased it on our mother's urging. "The best investment you'll ever make will be in the purchase of real estate." mom frequently said.

When I moved into the basement of the Burton house, my brother Dave and I spent hours putting up drywall over concrete block; texturing ceilings and wallpapering the half of the basement that was to be my living area. Dave was relocated by his company to Columbus, Ohio. He left the center apartment in 1984, and I purchased the home from him that same year.

I was working as a national educator for a chain hair salon, as well as working behind the chair full time as a cosmetologist. Being a single mom kept me busy in my non-paid-for profession, so

I had very little time for myself. The center apartment was the first floor of the home, which gave me a sense of added security because you can see the exterior entrances from anywhere on the first floor. I slept more restfully at night knowing this. Without a dog or a husband, I needed every safety advantage I could find.

Vincent was extremely precocious. I never spoke to him as though he were an infant, so his vocabulary at four was that of a child twice his chronological age. Because it was just the two of us the majority of the time, I would talk to Vince about my day at work and he would relate stories of his action- packed day at preschool. We would often do this while making dinner.

On one particular evening I'd made dinner alone. Vincent had become obsessed with a cartoon character named 'He-man' and his associated cronies. He loved to play pretend with these dolls and wasn't permitted to bring them to school, so I began frequently making allowances for him to have 'imagination time' instead of helping with dinner preparation.

As I tore salad at the kitchen sink, I called to Vince, "Get your hands washed for dinner!"

I heard what can best be described as a scurrying sound, almost like hard-soled shoes on a sandy, boarded surface. Stopping what I was doing, I twisted to my right to see Vince exiting the bathroom, his head down, attempting to pull the door closed behind him as he came into the hall. He was mumbling something as he struggled with the door. I stood there watching him, wet hands rummaging on the counter in front of me for a non-existent towel. Not taking my eyes off of him I asked, "Vincent, did you hear me tell you to wash your hands for dinner?"

He raised his head, looked at me with the most incredible soft blue eyes and quietly responded, "Yeah mom, I heard you."

He was acting peculiar.

"Then I suppose you washed your hands. Will they pass inspection?" I asked with a smile. This question never fails to get a response from my children, either negative or positive. It always brought smiles, however. He stared at me with no emotion.

"Vincent!" I gave him a minute to snap out of whatever he was mentally involved with, and then continued, "Who are you talking with?"

"Bacon".

A one -word response from the most talkative kid at school?
(And home.)

I knew single children often develop imaginary friends to keep them company. This was why I talked to Vince about my job, my day, the finances or whatever, so I was angry that he conjured one up in spite of my best efforts. "Well then," I said, "You'd better tell Bacon to wash his hands for dinner, too."

As he quickly and quietly walked past me through the kitchen to the table, head still down, he commented almost in a whisper, "Mom, ghosts don't eat."

Chapter Two

BACON at BURTON

David is the eldest in our family of eleven children. He was born in the post war baby boom of the fifties, reaching his teenage years in the turmoil of the sixties. Although he never finished his college degree, he has an enormous amount of savvy, street smarts, and intelligence. He has worked for several food service companies, as a successful self-employed entrepreneur, and currently as a manager of a home improvement store chain. He is the father of five beautiful daughters and numerous grandchildren. This is Dave's story as he related it to me and several witnesses. He refused to submit his story in writing because he didn't want to "conjure up" any memories of what happened, or invite any ghosts back into his life.

As a self-employed home improvement specialist, Dave often worked late and went to work early. One such night he arrived home after midnight, tired and filthy, wanting to shower in the basement so he wouldn't mess his family's main bathroom, and go to bed. It was July two thousand. As is common during the summers in Akron, the humidity was near eighty percent and the temperature hovered in the upper seventies even at this late hour. The weather had taken its toll on him. Even though he'd consider himself physically fit, he carried a few extra pounds on his five foot ten inch frame. He was a stocky football player in high school, and quite the ladies' man. All of this was irrelevant on this particular hot and humid summer night in Akron.

The lady he attracted this night wasn't the type he usually anticipated.

He, his wife and two youngest daughters lived on the third floor of the house that had been subdivided into three apartment's years before he'd purchased it. At the rear of the house is a set of interior stairs that divide the floors, with landings at each floor. After he finished showering in the basement, he ascended the first set of eight steps to the landing leading to the garage. He stopped briefly to make sure the door from the garage to the house was securely locked. As he turned to his right to go up the second flight of stairs he flicked the light switch off, leaving a hole of darkness behind him. The stairwell was illuminated by a single-bulb wall sconce, an original fixture dating from nineteen seventeen, when the house was built; it was electric, with fabric-coated wiring, common for the era. When the lights in the hall would flicker, as though they were about to go out, I attributed it to the age of the wiring.

 He ascended the next set of five steps to the first floor apartment, opening the door to his right, taking one step up onto the landing and turned around to lock the door behind him. He turned again to ascend the third set of seven stairs leading to a landing at the garage roof. This landing also has a door for easy exit in case of fire. As he turned to make the last set of eight stairs to the third floor, he glanced up to see what he thought was his wife at the top of the staircase. Yet
he knew this was an apparition; what he saw and what he knew to be true were obscured. This was common for others who have seen ghosts.

 The top floor hallway has the same incandescent wall sconce as the others in the back stairwell, whose light bulbs emit a yellowish light. The switch for the second floor hall light was at the very top of the stairs. Dave could very plainly see the woman standing, facing him. She was as solid-looking as you or I would be, standing at the top of the stairs looking down at him with an expressionless face.

 Dave smoked a cigarette as part of his nightly ritual; he'd lit one after his shower, smoking it as he made his way upstairs. His head was down to make sure that he didn't miss a step as he kept climbing, all the while thinking, 'my wife doesn't have brown hair...or a nightgown like that.' Yet he instinctively said aloud, with eyes still down, "Honey, I didn't mean to wake you."
He already began to feel the stickiness of humidity on his skin from the minimal exertion of climbing the stairs. As he lifted his

head to look up the staircase, he saw the woman walking away from him going down the hall, a total distance of twenty feet. As he reached the top of the steps and stood completely flat-footed and still, she turned and faced him once again. She was standing at the opposite end of the hall, looking directly at him. She never spoke or gestured, just stood silently staring into his eyes. He never felt emotion coming from her. She neither scared him nor made him pity her. She wasn't sad or happy, but completely devoid of emotion.

It was not his wife.

It was the ghost of a woman who would be seen by at least four other people visiting or living on Burton Avenue. Her skin is porcelain; pale skin similar to many Anglo Europeans. Her dark auburn hair hangs straight to just below her shoulders. Some have described it as more a reddish color, while others have described it as mousy brown. It depends on the light, I suppose. She's always seen wearing a white nightgown that falls to just above her ankle bone, but it could also be an undergarment. One person told me it looked like it was an eyelet lace pattern; scoop neck but not off the shoulders. A few who saw her told me that she is barefoot.

She is well groomed, leading me to believe she was a woman who was taken care of financially.

She is commonly described by others as "just plain looking", neither attractive nor homely, and appears very solid, not transparent or wispy as some ghosts are depicted. Everyone who has seen her thought another person had come into the house. She looks as real as the person next to you right now.

Dave said he actually thought someone had come into his house, perhaps an intruder. His thought simultaneously was that he knew he was seeing a ghost. While he was telling me about this incident, he held his cigarette out in front of him and said, "Then she dissipated, like the smoke from the end of my cigarette."

The house was once again eerily quiet and dark, with the exception of the dim light emitted from the wall sconce. Dave could feel the pounding of his heart in his ears. His wife and

daughters slept soundly; he didn't sleep very well at all. When I questioned him about his reaction to seeing a ghost he replied with his trademark grin, "I thought I'd have to take another shower because I really thought I shit myself. I actually had to reach around and check!"

The next morning he called Fr. Chima, a priest from nearby St. Sebastian Catholic Church, who set an appointment to come bless the house. Neither Dave nor the priest realized that this wasn't the first time that a Catholic priest had been called to this address.

Father Chima arrived a few days after the sighting. Dave described him as acting somewhat nervous, but he was composed and attentive once he entered the house. Father donned his stole before crossing the threshold, which is a long scarf worn around the neck by priests when they are performing a religious Ceremony, or Rite. He also brought his holy water, a powerful Sacramental used in numerous religious ceremonies.

Fr. Chima asked Dave to go through the house and make sure all doors and built-in drawers were open. Dave thought this was peculiar; he was also nervous and compensated by being humorous. He grinned a half smile and asked the priest, "So father, you think she'll try and hide?"

Father looked at him and firmly stated, "Possibly."

Father wasn't amused. He'd grown up in Africa with stories of possessions and evil entities. He knew what he could possibly be confronted with and he wasn't an exorcist, although parish priests are educated in the Rite of Exorcism.

He began praying in Latin, going through the house from room to room, sprinkling holy water from a small aspergillum throughout each room as he went. The blessing was perfunctory and completed in about thirty minutes. Fr. Chima told Dave to put a blessed crucifix above every entry door to his home as well. Dave was eager to oblige. The priest explained that he may need to return and told him as he stood in the threshold of the side door, "Often the blessings stop the situation from ever happening, but occasionally the ghost will appear again."

He told Dave to call him if he needed anything, said his goobye and left.

This was the first time in David's fifty-one year life that he felt compelled to call a priest. He was frightened by the experience, although the apparition itself wasn't frightening at all. At first he thought someone had broken in, yet simultaneously he knew what he was seeing was a ghost.

David told me this story in August of 2001 when I went back to Akron from Dallas to attend our brother Steven's wedding. Dave was nonchalant as he retold the tale, opening with "By the way... I saw a ghost at Burton."

Dave's demeanor is always that way. He is a matter-of-fact, proof positive kind of person. Well, he was up until that summer. A friend who was with me at the time said, "I never believed in ghosts until I met your family. There is just no way to doubt Dave's story when you hear him tell it."

I returned home to Dallas two days later. I sat outside my house on a stone bench with my grown son, Vincent, and we both smoked a cigarette and drank a beer while we story swapped.

Vincent was born in 1980 and we moved into the Burton house when he was just six months old. Ironically, my brother Dave owned the house then. I purchased it from him in 1984. David moved back in permanently in 1990 and has lived there ever since. I told Vince as we sat smoking that his Uncle Dave saw a ghost at Burton. Vince threw his head back, releasing a laugh with his smoke and asked, "Who did he see, Bacon or his daughter?"

I looked at him quizzically and said, "It was a girl, but what makes you think she's Bacon's daughter?"

"Because he told me." His response was without forethought or trepidation.

He was still looking up at the porch light, grinning at the thought of his uncle Dave being afraid of something.

"Who told you?" I asked.

I assumed his uncle Dave had called to let him know I was safely on my way home and told Vince of the incident. "Bacon."

He responded.

We sat for a minute or more in silence, sipping our beers, while I digested what he just said. Vince began to laugh, said he imagined Uncle Dave seeing a ghost and wished he could've been there to tease him about it; the two of them behave like fraternity brothers. "Remember when I'd wake up in the middle of the night talking?" Vincent asked me.

"It didn't happen in the middle of the night, it was always eleven o'clock, straight up."

I remember well, but never imagined that Vincent would have any recollection of it; he was only five years old! I was surprised when he said, "Well, Bacon would come and talk to me. He told me that he was asked to assist in the Underground Railroad by John Brown."

Bacon owned one of the largest parcels of land in what is now West Akron, aside from Simon Perkins.

"Bacon believed in the cause and kept runaway slaves in the basement of his house. One night, the people in town found out what he was doing and burned his house to the ground. Bacon and his daughter died in the fire."

He stopped to take a long drag from his cigarette, then continued, "They kept slaves in what is now the storage room of the basement, just below the kitchen, which was originally the coal chute."

He had no way of knowing this as a child. "Sometimes at night you can hear faint songs from that room, like slave songs. They sang even as they died."

Vincent shifted from side to side on his concrete bench, looking like he was trying to get comfortable. He took another long drag from his cigarette, staring solemnly into the darkness from the front porch.

"You never told me." I was perplexed and intrigued. I also felt a bit ashamed at having waited fifteen years to talk to my son about this.

"Why do you think I was so upset when you decided to put my playroom in the basement?" He exclaimed in a shrill voice.

I'd completely forgotten about the fit he threw when he came home from school one day to see that I'd switched his playroom from his first floor bedroom to the basement level. I never understood why he wouldn't be happy with having more room to play. He never told me there were ghosts down there!

"By the way, she was pregnant." He continued, "Sometimes you may hear of a mother waking up to hear her baby crying, even though her baby is sound asleep." He paused before adding, "Or unborn."

He asked me if that had ever happened to any of the tenants there. I've been unable to locate any of them to ask. There have only been two who lived there with small children or babies.

By this time I was dumbfounded. I also began to recall incidents that happened when we'd lived there, things I'd long since dismissed as coincidence or a frazzled mind and body. Like the night a bearded, older man wearing a long trench coat stood at the bottom of my bed. I woke with the sensation I was being observed, yet felt no alarm when I saw him. I was tired after working twelve hours; I rolled over and went back to sleep. I recall thoughts being conveyed between this bearded apparition and myself, but can't recall the content, with the exception of my thinking 'leave me alone, I need sleep'. I do remember that I felt no fear. Most women who work full time and have a child or children know how exhausted I was at eleven o'clock. Not even a ghost could make me get out of my comfy bed!

"You won't find a deed between 1856 and 1917 either." Vincent shocked me when he offered that bit of information. He had no way of knowing I'd already researched the deed and he was right on; but we'll get into that later in the book.

I asked anyway, "Why not?"

"No one wanted to rebuild the house after what happened. It was only after Akron began to explode and the land became increasingly valuable that it was sold, in 1916."

The property had in fact been sold to a Mr. Fairhead, whose wife, Irene told me her husband had purchased the land in 1916 and built a house on it for her as a wedding gift, which was completed in 1917. This was later confirmed when the house was sold to me. She confided to my older sister, Dolores, that her daughter died of a drug overdose while at home, and that she'd outlived three husbands and all but one of her five children. Irene passed away in 1988.

Vincent and I talked for a while afterwards about my brother's wedding and what happened at home in Dallas while I was away. We went inside, it was late and we went to bed. We both admitted the next day that the ghost conversation weighed heavily on our minds, and we both had a difficult time getting to sleep that night.

His story did give me the impetus to research thoroughly, and to begin the journey into the family connection to the paranormal.

I began by researching John Brown. It was a difficult task as there was nothing in the Ohio Historical Society about him. I contacted them and a wonderful volunteer, Erin, e-mailed to let me know that John Brown's home was grouped under the Erie Canal Historical Society. It wasn't enough information, however, so on a lark I decided to check the internet under 'abolitionist.' Bingo. My hair stood on ends as I saw the architectural similarities between his home and the Burton house. Both wooden houses were recently aluminum sided in the same Cape Cod grey vinyl siding with white trim, both built late nineteenth or early twentieth century; frame houses with gables and a huge front porch. Mr. Brown's scraggly beard and overall facial features remarkably resembled Bacon's; described to me a hundred times from people who saw him. He also bore an uncanny resemblance to the apparition that stood at the bottom of my bed twenty-some years prior. Seeing the photo is what jogged my memory of that night. What I found most intriguing was that John Brown was hanged and died in Harper's Ferry, West Virginia on December second- Vincent's birthday.

Vincent himself was somewhat taken aback when I told him this. Perhaps it's because Vince abhors injustice, so was actually being contacted by John Brown. Maybe because he was a child, and could lend an ear to an old man who had no one to listen to him in this world.

Whatever the ghost's reason, he chose Vince to relate his story to. I dismissed the notion that it was Mr. Brown because despite the similarities, he told my son his name was Bacon. He also managed to scare the daylights out of Vince and several tenants while I was living there. The following took place at the Burton house in 1985:

Her name is being withheld as I've been unable to locate her, so I'll refer to her as Lois.

Lois and I were co-workers at a local hair salon. I had been a single mother for years, often selecting roommates to assist with the enormous utility bills that are the downside of owning a large house. Lois was easy going, quick to laugh and professional on the job. Vince was young, they got along, and she contributed not only financially but emotionally to my single-parent household; we became good friends.

Lois was in her early twenties and this was her first time to live away from her parents' home. She visited her family frequently, but relished her independence. I couldn't tell you how long Lois had lived with us, perhaps seven months. One night she was awakened by a bearded man who was standing at the foot of her bed. She later told me she had the sensation she was being watched as she slept, and that sensation is what woke her. The same feeling I'd had, yet I'd never told her what happened to me. This time however, the ghost told Lois to "Get out!" while forcefully yanking the comforter off of her bed.

Around three in the morning I was awakened by an excruciatingly loud, shrill scream. I threw my blankets aside, raced to the front of the house, and saw her standing at the headboard of her queen-sized bed, clutching her rose-printed sheet to her chest. She was pale, eyes wide open.

She was perspiring and trembling as though she'd been doused with ice water. Vince was at the opposite side of her headboard, just outside his bedroom door. As I rounded the corner I heard him say, "Lois, it's just Bacon. He won't hurt you."

I immediately became angry and yelled at my son, "Enough about this damn Bacon, ghost don't exist, now go to bed!"

He looked at me and I knew I'd hurt his feelings, yet I was upset that he would be confirming her fears. I was sick of all the talk about ghosts at my house, it made prospective renters nervous. I was beginning to think perhaps my son made Bacon up in his mind to get attention.

I put my arm around Lois' shoulder and directed her over to the couch, although she was reluctant to leave her spot in the corner of the bedroom and resisted me at first. She sat on the couch and started to cry, then began relating information so fast I could barely make out what she was saying. I took a seat next to her, she was leaning hard into me, crying and shaking uncontrollably. We were in the middle of the room facing the fireplace, her bed behind us. When she calmed down somewhat, I stood and slowly walked the perimeter of the room while listening to her, rechecking all of the windows and doors. The Burton house had been built like a fortress.

The window casements are solid oak, and I had replaced the picture windows on each side of the main door with bullet-proof glass. The windows on either side of the fireplace were about six feet off the ground and narrow, with built-in book shelves below with glass doors. Anyone attempting to enter that way would make enough noise to wake the neighborhood. When I finished I walked back to her and said, "No one can get in this place."

She immediately jumped into a standing position, looked me straight in the eyes and hissed, "Someone did tonight! He threw my covers on the floor, look at them!"

She pointed to a heap of fabric lying at the foot of her bed. "He told me to get out, and that's exactly what I'm going to do!"

I tried for the next several hours to get her to reconsider. I brought her a beer from the refrigerator to calm her nerves. She had her boyfriend's truck, loaded and ready to go, by seven o'clock in the morning; just over four hours from the first and only time she ever saw Bacon.

What she described was a man about six feet tall, wearing a long black coat, possibly a duster she said. He was about sixty years old, with a weathered face and scraggly beard. When she was first awakened, he was staring at her, and she rubbed her eyes, thinking she may be dreaming. Like Dave, she first thought it could be an intruder, yet subconsciously she knew what he was.

He wasn't transparent either. He yelled at her and physically moved her bedding.

Lois and I continued to work together for years after she left Burton, but she refused to talk about what happened that morning. She still resides in the Akron area but I haven't had any luck in trying to locate her.

Shortly after purchasing Burton, I took classes in Real Estate. I passed the exam and began working for my mother's real estate company; she retired as one of three owners of Ghent Realty in Bath, Ohio.

One day while I was at the office, a coworker asked if I'd accompany him to the title office in downtown Akron to research a listing he'd recently acquired. I agreed and off we went. I wanted to research the Burton property, so this was my golden opportunity. The realtors name was Mike O'Donnell, my sister Cecilia's brother-in-law. We drove the fifteen or so miles on highway 77 from our office, picking up highway 59 into downtown Akron. After exiting we made a right onto High Street and began looking for an open parking meter. The dreary morning had given way to a steady rain, so we opted to park in the High Street garage, close to our destination.

Once in the records building, I immediately went to the files, alphabetically organized by street name and found Burton rather quickly. I couldn't find a deed prior to 1917, and was certain a house existed on that parcel years before then. As I was looking, a sandy- blonde male in his early twenties approached me and asked if he could be of assistance. I told him what I was looking for, that I couldn't find a deed prior to 1917. He said, "You won't find a deed that old up here. We keep all the old ones downstairs. I'll show you where to find them."

He then escorted me to the elevators and into the basement. As we exited the elevator, I followed him as he took a right down a short hall, and entered room on the left lined with file cabinets. I thanked him and he exited. The large room was adequately lit with incandescent bulbs in old metal, pan-like ceiling fixtures. It was lined with metal filing cabinets and had a musty smell of old paper. I eventually found the deed for the property, but what I read sent chills up and down my spine. I stood staring at the yellowed paper in my hands, not able to move. There was a gap of almost forty years where the land stood vacant. I slowly looked around to see if anyone was watching me, then bolted for the elevators. My heart was racing as fast as my mind; with fingers shaking I pressed the 1 elevator button, returning to the first floor for what seemed like an eternity. I was unnerved and fought hard psychologically to contain myself. I saw Mike halfway across the room as I exited the elevators. I walked to him in record speed, shoved the papers into his hand and said, "Read this!"

His eyes got no further than the first line which described the parcel as 'Bacon; Lot all...' He looked at me rather perplexed and said, "Isn't Bacon the name of Vincent's imaginary friend?"

"Yes!" I replied.

"Well, did it ever occur to you that maybe his imaginary friend isn't imaginary?"

Duh! I thought.

"Yes it did, as soon as I read the property description. I need to get out of here."

We both needed to get out of there as quickly as possible; Mike was due back at the office and I was shaking so hard the papers were rattling in my hand. Because you're not allowed to remove the original deeds from the city offices, I took them to an employee to have a copy made. I told the girl in the plexi-glass cubicle to thank the young man who'd helped me locate the files. She stated flatly, "We don't have anyone to help you. If someone did, they were just being nice."

Chills ran the length of my spine for the second time that day. I turned to Mike and asked as my eyes scanned the room, "Do you see the young boy that helped me?"

I wanted to thank him verbally and monetarily.

"Sue, I never saw you talking with anyone here."

This was the first inkling I had that there were people other than the living variety at the Burton address and possibly in this building.

Everything began to make sense; Lois had in fact seen the ghost of this man 'Bacon', as did I. My young son was communicating with him, and had been for years!

Chapter 3

DANCING in DENVER

Dolores (Dee) and Mark divorced shortly after moving into
their home in North Denver. They lived all over the world
because of Mark's position in the Air Force. Dee was a devoted
wife and mother of three, always ready to assist her husband in
whatever way she was needed to promote his career. As anyone
who's married to a career military person will attest to, the
moves are constant with sometimes very little notice.

Dee is perhaps best described as laid back by those that know
her well. She's not rattled easily unless her children or loved
ones are in danger, then she's as vicious as a grizzly bear. She
also grew up during the turmoil of the sixties, and has
experienced personal emotional pain that most of us could only
imagine. I won't divulge what the personal trauma was out of
respect for my sister and her family. She is one of the kindest and
most generous people I have ever known.

Her ex-husband Mark retired and moved the family to a Denver
suburb. Shortly after they arrived at the old farm house on Gun
Club Drive he permanently left Dee and their three children;
Cecilia, Mark and Catherine. She confided to me in a phone
conversation, "I think he put me in the middle of the boon docks
intentionally."

He only thought he'd left her and the children alone in the old
farm house. Soon after moving into her new residence, one of
several in the past ten years, Dee went to bed tired, but not
exhausted as she had been so often lately. This night she read for
a while to tire her eyes, as she usually does prior to sleeping.
After a short time, perhaps fifteen minutes, she rolled to her
right to turn out the light on her nightstand. She would remain on
her right side as she fell asleep, with pillow tucked tightly
between her extended right arm and her head.

Just before dozing off, she felt the mattress behind her dip slightly under the weight of an unknown partner, causing her to rock momentarily and tilt slightly towards the center of her queen bed. She felt pressure on her back and thought perhaps one of her children had decided to lie next to her throughout the night. She also knew it wasn't one of her children. She lie awake, eyes wide open and senses on heightened alert until fatigue overcame her. She was "paralyzed with fear" and later told me that she was "too scared to scream." It was so traumatic, in fact, that she asked me to tell the story. Dee still becomes visibly upset when she recalls that first sensation of spirits being with her. This particular incident caused Dee to begin her search for another home. She felt as though the 'other people' in her house were becoming bold, bold enough to touch them. She didn't realize at the time how right she was, because they were getting bolder, and they had just begun.

The following story was e-mailed to me by Dee; I am rewriting it exactly as she sent it, as I was unable to copy this story onto my text:

My exposure to the spiritual world began in Colorado and occurred between Oct. 1998 and June 2001. That is the best time line I can give since I know it happened after Mark left but before I got a waterbed in my room. I was reading in bed and it was still the "regular" mattress. I felt pressure at my feet and thought one of the cats had jumped up on my bed, as I was lowering my book I said, "What do you think you're doing, you know you're not allowed in my room!", but by that time I had lowered the book and could see there was nothing at the bottom of the bed even though I could still feel the pressure. I just slowly put the book back over my face and said, "OK but just stay on your own side of the bed."

Some may argue this was psychological trauma caused from the divorce; I disagree because pressure as though someone was on her bed happened more than once. Her bedroom was where the first incident happened as well. There was definitely negative energy in her room.

Scientifically, there is no way a mattress can move unless force is put upon it.

Back to Dee's original story:

After I got the waterbed I was moving my queen size mattress and box springs to Catherine's room down the hall. Cath helped me move the mattress, but it wouldn't stay standing against the wall without falling, so I told her to just hold it- I would try to get the box springs by myself. I was able to move it fine but when I got through the doorway to her room I physically felt the other end of the box springs get lighter and thought Cath had found a way to keep the mattress from falling and had come to help me. I finished putting the box springs against the other wall and turned to thank Catherine. She was still at the opposite wall holding the mattress- just smiled at me and said, "it wasn't me mom!"

I woke up one night and wasn't sure what woke me, then heard what sounded like someone running across the mother-in-law quarters roof, which you could access from the main house second floor windows. There was no one on the roof- and I went out on the balcony and didn't see anyone in the area, or a car leaving, or an animal. Where my house was situated the balcony faced the front of the house towards the road so anyone leaving by vehicle I could easily see. My daughter, Celia, told me she often heard what she thought was footsteps on the roof when she lived in the mother-in-law quarters.

I explored the possibility that this could be caused by animals jumping from trees that surround the house. When I questioned Dee, Celia and Catherine about this possibility, they all said they thought the same thing at first, but never heard the thud from an animal jumping onto the roof, or saw or heard an animal or person leaving. More from Dolores:

 I came home one night around 2AM and entered through the main house front door. I heard what sounded like voices from a large group of people and thought Celia had friends over. I went over to the mother-in-law quarters to say Hi since I knew most of her friends, but there was no one there- the voices stopped when I opened the door from my kitchen into her living room. I checked and both Celia and her daughter, Briana, were both asleep and there was no TV on.
 My son Mark came home late one night and was fixing himself something to eat. The pantry was a walk-in and was to your right when you were facing the stove. He started to cook eggs, but noticed the light on in the pantry, he turned the light off and continued cooking. He saw, out of his peripheral vision the light come back on. No one else was up at the time and couldn't have gone to the pantry without being seen. Mark just turned off the stove and decided he wasn't that hungry after all and went to bed.
 Catherine, my youngest daughter, had a friend, Vanessa, spend the night. They were sleeping in the living room so they could watch TV. Catherine was on the loveseat facing the TV and her girlfriend was facing towards the fireplace. In the middle of the night Vanessa woke up to see a little girl sitting cross-legged in the fireplace. She tried to scream to wake up Catherine but no sound would come out of her mouth. She told Catherine she would never come back to our house…could visit somewhere else.

 I remember Dee telling me this story the day after it happened. She said Vanessa's father came to pick her up from the house shortly after receiving an urgent phone call from his daughter in the middle of the night. He was irate that Dee did not disclose the fact that she had ghosts at her house before his daughter spent the night.

Brianna was still sleeping in the bedroom in the mother-in-law quarters and told her mom that her great-grandad had come to visit her. She was two when he died and she had never met him. She told us he came to visit and told her he loved her. When it was time for him to go she told him she didn't want him to go but he said, "I need to go back and be...I wanted you to know I love you." Bri told us there were other "people" in her closet that wanted her to go with them. She had a picture of my paternal grandfather and told me that is who came to see her. Bri wanted a picture of my grandfather on her nightstand for months.

Dee had numerous events such as these, and when I e-mailed her to ask if I could use her stories as she related she agreed, then added the following response:

"There was also an incident when I was at the house myself when moving where the step-stool hit me hit me in the back." She continued, "I didn't say anything because I didn't want to "plant" an idea, but then she got hit in the back when she was over there by herself. She said it felt like someone's fist in the small of her back and she thought at first maybe the broom had fallen on her since she was bent over cleaning the half bath, but nothing was around her. Also, when we were there upstairs the last night she saw a group walk by the bottom of the stairs- she didn't say anything other than "mom let's just go-whatever is left here they can have."

I spoke with Celia after she was 'hit'. She explained that one reason she went back to the house alone was to get her pet cat.

The second was to clean so the family could receive their security deposit. Dee's story takes over from the point where Celia was scrubbing the floor. She had been there about an hour. The cat was in the hallway behind her and had arched its back, hissed, and ran off just before the incident occurred. Celia left immediately, not looking back once to retrieve her cat.

This is what gives credence to the story. This ardent animal lover was frightened to the point of leaving her beloved cat to fend for itself. The cat sensed someone else there also. Celia and Dee did go back the following day to get her pet, and felt great remorse for leaving her cat in the first place.

Dee continued with her messages to me:

"The day I saw Celia walking down the hallway away from the wet bar towards the front door and called out to her and started to follow, she came into the kitchen from the mother-in-law quarters behind me so there was no way it could have been her I saw.

When I went into the hallway no one was there. She also went into the upstairs bedroom, the one in the north-east corner, and saw her reflection in the mirror-definitely a spirit there that looks a lot like my daughter- long dark hair and a younger person.

Celia saw what most folks believe to be what ghosts look like-the misty entity of undefined- gender is more a feeling or intuition rather than a visual sighting. Where I saw what I thought was my daughter, she saw the misty forms that dissipated around what would be knee level. She saw a "female" (as I said more of an intuition) in the doorway going from the mother-in-law quarters into the main house kitchen, and another time the "male" entity in the living room next to the fireplace.

The landlord told me he was in the house once by himself and went to leave and glanced back and saw a whole group dancing on the dance floor. He said he just left and closed the door behind him."

I had the pleasure of visiting Dee at her home on Gun Club Road. After an exhausting fifteen hour drive from Dallas, my family and I arrived shortly after six o'clock Denver time. My sister wasn't home from work, but my nieces Celia and Catherine were there to greet my four children and me. After many hugs and kisses, we went into the house.

I was shocked at how disorderly her house looked and I immediately began a cleaning crusade. My sister worked a full-time job and went to school, leaving precious little time for the tedium of housework; that is what sisters are for; to visit and clean! After cleaning the kitchen pantry, I moved onto the half bath on the first floor off the main hall, a short distance from the front door. Dee came in, jubilant not only to see me, but to see her home being cleaned. (Is this not every single working mother's fantasy?).

She put on a pot of coffee. The time was spent shouting from kitchen to hall about our drive to Denver, her day at work, and the usual queries one has as a guest in a family home. As she was telling me about her graduate classes, I interrupted her to let her know that she was out of toilet paper in her lavatory.

"I just went to the commissary," she replied. "I put a case on the inside of the basement stairwell."

I went to the basement and pulled the door, only to find it was off its hinges. I leaned it against the door jamb leading into the kitchen and told her, "This is something else I need to fix while I'm here." We both laughed.

I heard the children in the basement making noise and shouted to them to bring me the toilet paper, which had fallen to the bottom of the stairwell. Because I had surgery twice for a severe break on my right ankle, going up and down steps is extremely painful for me. I got no response from them, but could hear their voices down there. Once again I shouted, "Bring up the toilet paper!"

Once again I got no response. Just as I began calling individual names, Dee came from the kitchen to my right, gently pushing my right shoulder, causing me to stumble into the opening of the living room on my left, where I saw my four children, Dee's two daughters and her granddaughter engrossed in a movie on television. I looked at Dee and asked, "If they're in there, who's down there?" pointing to the basement.

She placed the loose door over the chasm to the basement and said, "That's what I heard the night I came home from work. It sounds like someone's having a party, but no one's there."

I told her I hope she had plenty of napkins, because there was no way I was going to venture down to retrieve her toilet paper!

Although she'd heard these same sounds before in different parts of the house and at different times, she heard nothing as we stood at the top of those stairs on that hot July evening.

What makes these stories so unusual is that Dee lived for a time at Burton Avenue in Akron, a place that had numerous ghost sightings, yet she never saw or experienced anything strange there. When the ghosts began arriving in her Denver home and she realized they were spirits, she mistakenly thought perhaps they had followed her from Burton.

Dolores has thought several times that she has spirits that 'follow her', and I believe that it's a possibility. She has an unwavering love of Christ and family. She also has a devotion to the blessed Mother of God's Rosary and prays it daily, encouraging others to do the same. Spirits know that a close union with Dee results in getting closer to God through her intercessory prayer. The evil spirits are working overtime on the opposing side, constantly feeding her fears in a diabolical tug-of-war for her soul. The more frequently she prays, the more the nasty ghosts' torment her. In Dee's case, Mr. Nasty Casper has to first get past Mary and her besties, the dominion of angels.

Spirits can attach themselves to a person only if the person's will allows them entry. Dee, through prayer and devotion to the Eucharist (which Catholics believe is the true physical, spiritual, actual Body of Christ, Our Lord) is guaranteed protection from evil.

Doesn't mean they can't scare the hell out of you trying, though!

We know now that these spirits were in Denver the entire time. Too many others, including a former owner and landlord, saw and heard the ghosts at the Gun Club address.

Dolores' children, now grown with families of their own, still reside in the greater Denver area.

My computer has done several strange things as I write these events. It repeated the last line of the chapter I wrote regarding Dolores and her children, 'They moved from the house on Gun Club Rd. in October 2005,' at least seventeen times. The number of times the line is repeated changes every time I got into Word Documents. Tonight my computer shut down completely then returned exactly where I'd left off. The screen went totally black for about four seconds; it's never done that before, or since. Normally if it shuts down it will restart, and sometimes you can lose the entire text. I'll pray before retiring that I don't lose the book, or my mind! I have copied several e-mails between my sister Dolores, her daughter Cecilia and myself. These were some that would transfer for me:

Flag this message

RE: Aunt Sue

Wednesday, December 13, 2006 11:03 AM

From: Cecelia

If I remember anymore, I will send it off. What was odd is that I tried to send the document to me four times before it went through. It kept telling me I didn't have enough memory to send the email. Just strange things, I am very happy I am out of that house.

Celia's email never came through to me in its entirety, just this last paragraph. I've never received a 'partial' email before or since. One of my technical assistants told me that it was impossible, "They either come through or they don't."

In a phone conversation with me later, she explained that her email was about the smell of smoke she experienced in the house, which Dee responded to below:

Sent: Wednesday, December 13, 2006 10:01 AM
Cc: Cecelia

Subject: FW: Aunt Sue

Hi Celia - done deal.

Hi Sue,

Celia sent this to you. After reading hers it reminded me of times when I smelled smoke too - I went so far as to go into the basement thinking there was a fire down there and the smoke was coming up through the vent in the hallway half-bathroom. I could smell it but I didn't see smoke. Never found a real fire either. Now that we are out of there, my fear was history was going to repeat itself and there was going to be another fire - always scared me when I smelled the smoke. I forgot too about Bri talking about great-great grandma that spoke French - did she? I told Celia I know my maternal grandmother was French/Irish but didn't know if she spoke the language. After Celia read about me hearing running across the roof she was relieved - "mom, you heard it too?" Almost as if she did believe she was going crazy. I also heard the drums but "blamed" them too on neighbors and sound traveling at night - even though it did sound as if it was right outside the door - flippin Indian drumming - like the other noises I would hear - if I went to find the source the sound moved or stopped. I smelled the smoke in the front hallway but Celia almost felt as if she was "invaded" - told me her girlfriend, Jessica, was over once when it happened to her...she smelled the smoke and felt disoriented, (told me it felt like she was living someone else's memory) and Jess told

her she got real pale and was unresponsive to her.

**Let the fun continue!! Glad we are finally out of there.
Think I already told you but I asked Bri about our new
house and if she liked living there or missed the old one
(since she had lived there since birth) and she told me, "I like
our new house better grandma, no one else lives in it!"
Maybe I will remember more - or maybe not!!!! Love you
sis, Dee**

(Brianna's great, great grandmother, Mary Poulain-Genevie
spoke fluent French).

I believe Brianna is a visionary as well as an adorable great
niece.

Her mother, my niece Cecilia was driving her daughter to a
fellow kindergartener's birthday party. They'd stopped at the
neighborhood Walmart store to purchase a gift, gift bag and
tissue paper for the five year old birthday girl's party. When they
left the store, Cecilia placed Bri in her car seat on the passenger
side of the car so she could turn and see her child from the
driver's seat as she talked.

At the stop light just out of the plaza parking lot was a bus stop.
As she waited for the light to turn green, Cecilia looked to her
right beyond the empty front passenger seat and noticed an
elderly woman sitting on the bench, evidently waiting for her
bus. Brianna looked out her window at the woman, too. Then
looked at her mom and said, "Isn't that a beautiful angel,
mommy?"

Celia was moved with appreciation to God that her daughter
could see the divine presence in such a woman, who to her
looked poor, dirty and downtrodden. The light changed and as
she accelerated from the stop she briefly turned to smile at her
daughter and said, "Honey, you are so precious for thinking of
that old woman as an angel."

Brianna tipped her head to one side and scrunched her nose in
disapproval. "Mommy, that old lady wasn't an angel. The angel
was standing behind her!"

Celia told me she almost wrecked the car.

I remember Celia telling me about the day she was home alone, waiting for the plumber to come replace their water heater. She'd taken Brianna to daycare and everyone else was at work. Dee was relieved that she wouldn't have to miss a day of work to wait for a plumber and could take a relaxing, warm bath when she got home that evening.

The plumber arrived surprisingly close to when he said he would. Celia left the kitchen where she was doing dishes when she saw the truck pull in the drive, and met him at the front door. She showed him through the center hall to the basement door, and told him where to find the water heater once he got in the basement. She went back to the kitchen and called her mother to tell her the plumber had arrived. She no sooner put the phone back in its cradle that she heard the plumber running up the rickety wooden steps from the basement. She arrived at the kitchen doorway at the center hall and he'd already beaten her to the front door. He was out of the house, down the steps of the front patio, and in his truck within seconds. She shouted to him as he flung his truck door open, "Did you fix the water heater?" "No ma'am. The man in the basement told me to leave."
He shouted this as he flung his truck door open, jumped in and turned the ignition on, then abruptly twisted his body to look out the back window. Celia shouted back, "There's no man in the basement, I'm here alone!"
He turned to her long enough to yell, "No you ain't!"
As he gunned the truck in reverse onto the street, leaving a cloud of dust wafting to her on the front porch, before slamming his truck into drive and kicking up more dust as he raced away.
Celia walked back into the house. "Shit." She said aloud as she slapped her arms down to her sides, "I'm stinky and dusty and can't take a shower, and now I'm stuck here with a damn ghost."

She called her mother who in turn immediately called the plumbing company and spoke with the owner.
"No ma'am, he refuses to go back to that house. Said there's the ghost of a man in the basement don't want him there. He was scared to death when he got back here. He's worked for me for

years, and I've never seen him in such a state, but I can't make him go back."

Dee thought about what the man just said, then measuredly answered, "Really? You're telling me that your employee, says a ghost, residing in my home, told him to leave?"

She spoke very slowly and deliberately, a technique designed and refined by our dear mother, Mary Jane. (She told us that it naturally causes people to desire to hear more of what you have to say, and to think about what they have just said). Dee went on in her extreme business voice, (also a Mary Jane speaking technique), "Just to clarify, you won't fix my water heater because your employee is afraid of a ghost?"

How ludicrous a question is that?

The line was quiet for a few seconds, then she heard him chuckling as he said, "No ma'am, I never said I wouldn't fix your water heater. I said I can't get my man to go back there. He just flat won't do it, no reasoning with him."

("That guy's really on the ball!" Mom would've said about this man, then would wink at us. She was a gifted manipulator, in a good way.)

The owner came over later that day, after normal business hours, and fixed the water heater without incident for Dee.

From: DOLORES

Sent: Tuesday, December 12, 2006 8:12 AM

To: 'SUSAN

Subject: RE: family connections

I always got weirded out too - not sure what ever happened in that house on Gun Club - I know the original burnt to the ground but it has always been strange to me that there is an entire party going on - only experiences with four different entities that I'm aware of but the male and female Celia saw, the little girl Catherine's friend Vanessa saw, and the

young lady that looked like Celia I saw - different than the

one Celia saw. Still strange to me that what I saw looked "human" but Celia saw the wispy entities that common belief is that is what a ghost looks like. Bri saw her great-granddad which was a comfort but the others she saw scared me because they told her they wanted her to go with them. That's when we moved her bedroom and took her upstairs close to me. She ended up with them there too - came into my room one night and asked me if we had ghosts, "grandma, there are people in my closet that talk weird like this", and then her voice went real low and raspy.....I had her get in my bed and off grandma went with the holy water - told "them" to leave her the f... alone or I'm gonna run you out!!!!! That's when I told them to get in the basement and stay there. They seemed to "listen" for a while but I still cannot believe I lived in that house so long. Then when we were going to go to the reunion in '99 both Bri and Celia came and got in my bed the night before we were leaving.

The bedroom door blew shut and I couldn't open it - even took off the hinges - I had tools in my bedroom since I was fixing things, since my room had the balcony with the window to the bedroom next to it we called Cath on her cell phone (thank God for cell phones) and she opened the window so Celia could get out of the room - she was starting to loose it - then the two of them pushed on my door and it still wouldn't open. I told them to kick the fu....r in!!!!

I forgot about that - still need to continue remembering events. I think I blocked many to save my sanity!!!!!!!

I remember you and I on the phone at times too and we could talk for hours about anything else but once we began talking about the "spirits" there would be static on the line or it would go dead. All I can say is God protected me - mentally and physically!!! I KNEW you would get the do, do, do do!!!!! Glad it gave you a laugh!!

Love you sis. Talk soon!! Finals this week and I'm free again!!!!!!

From: SUSAN

Sent: Tuesday, December 12, 2006 7:23 AM

To: DOLORES

Subject: RE: family connections

Those types of things have been happening all through this process; I'm now paying more attention to it- and have one of the diaconate understudies praying for me. He's helping with some of the church teachings and has turned me onto some great info. (which you and I will have to share over coffee someday) The day after I e-mailed you and cc'd myself, the book was gone from word. Both Dave and I checked, and it was nowhere to be found- as though it was never there. Kids swear it wasn't them; they weren't on the computer as they reminded me. I pray my rosary- pray the seven sorrows as well. (My priest) told me to stay close to the Sacraments, which I am. But some of this stuff is weirding me out. According to all I've read and been told by my deacon friends and priest I have every reason to be cautious. No power over us, but weird. I'm gonna have a great day.... you do the same!
PS-lol when I read do do do do.....HEE HEE!

" DOLORES" <DOLORES> wrote:

Thank you sis!! I am going to save the attachment to a disk and see if I can add to it - that way I won't "destroy" your original. Want to hear another "weird" experience - this email went directly to my "junk" folder and the only reason I "found" it today is I haven't been able to send emails because I'm over limit so I was cleaning up everything. This is the ONLY email of yours that had not come to my inbox directly - do, do, do, do!!!!!!!!!!
Love you sis!!

As I tried again to copy a few more of Dolores's emails, my laptop refused to open them. The prompt stated: 'The last time this document was opened it caused an error.' What an understatement!

A few weeks after the book 'disappeared' from the computer, it reappeared. I've been ready to throw the towel in several times, but feel compelled to get this story out. The more I talk about it with friends, clients and family, the more stories I hear. If you're experiencing paranormal events, you're not alone.

My sister Dolores's e-mails and electronic correspondence are the only ones that have given me trouble. I have spoken to all family members, conducting lengthy interviews over the phone and via the internet with no problem. Mine are the only ones that have given her problems as well.

The house on Gun Club Drive in Denver; taken in 2004 during my visit there. It has since been razed.

Dolores answered her door one early Saturday morning to a young woman who told her that she was in town for her high school reunion. She explained to Dee that she'd grown up in the old farmhouse, and wanted to reminisce a bit. Dee invited her in, but the woman explained that she was in a hurry, and couldn't stay long. Dee asked her if she or her family ever had problems with ghosts, and the girl offered some intriguing information. She said that her family never had problems, but told Dee that she'd heard the original farm house had burned to the ground during a Christmas party in the early part of the twentieth century.

According to this girl's story, the candles on the Christmas tree ignited it, and from its location in the living room, it trapped the occupants inside, killing them all. (Live candles on a Christmas tree were a common practice before the electric light bulb). Dee, regretfully, didn't get the woman's name, so I was unable to get an interview, but I believe that's the 'party' several of us have heard in the old farm house.

As far as the 'drumming' sound, the entity that resembled Celia, (very dark, almost black straight hair and eyes as dark as coal), and the little Indian girl in the fireplace; I think the house was situated on what was once an Indian reservation, due to its location. It doesn't explain all of the paranormal activity they experienced while living there, but it explains a lot of the occurrences.

Fear can escalate in a person causing them to become physically ill; welts can develop on the skin from anxiety, but that wasn't the case with the entity that struck Celia at the Denver house. She was physically assaulted. Poltergeists are known for this type of behavior, and have done so several times in the books I've read. None of the family members brought up in the book were afraid of anything at the time of the sightings. They were living their lives as normal, doing household tasks. Celia in particular, although uncomfortable being alone in the house, was trying to clean the lavatory floor when she was hit. Dave had just taken a shower and was looking forward to a good night's sleep. No one wanted to experience what they did, or see what they saw. The spiritual world has its own agenda, and we live in their world, not the other way around as we perceive it to be.

In one of the several books on exorcism that I read while researching this book, one author cites no biblical documentation for exorcising a house. He does admit that it is often 'fruitful' however, using the same prayers that are used for humans. He also states that he never witnessed the manifestation of a spirit in human form; that often the squeaks and thumps we hear in old places create the anxiety and fear we feel; that our mind 'conjures up' these ghosts.

I know for a fact that no one who came forward in this book tried to conjure up anything, but I understand that sometimes people think there are ghosts present, when in actuality there is often a simple explanation.

When ghosts don't appear as they did when they were with their bodies, they can often be seen as 'orbs'; balls of milky white light, similar to what Cecelia saw. I've seen orbs in numerous family photos, on a variety of cameras. Sometimes they appear as 'wisps' of light; or dark like a shadow.

Several years ago while I was on a break at work, I saw a very dark entity following a client to her car as she left the salon. It looked as if her shadow was upright, maybe ten inches behind her, tracing her steps behind her as she walked. She got into her car and the shadow disappeared into the car with her. She saw me and a co-worker who was enjoying the outdoors with me staring at her, so she smiled at us as she backed her car out of the parking space. I smiled weakly back at her and we waved goodbye. The entity frightened me because I sensed it was malevolent. The coworker, sitting next to me on a bench, looked at me and from her expression I knew she'd seen it, too. "You saw that, didn't you?" I asked.

She was holding a soda in her right hand which she lifted and while holding onto the can, pointed her index finger in the direction of the exiting car, "The darkness that's following that woman? Yep I did."

It was incredibly wonderful to know someone else could see what I was seeing, and she was equally happy to find a friend who understood and believed her.

We discussed whether this person could tell she was being followed by some very negative force or not. We thought about telling her or her stylist, but when it comes to this subject matter, too many people are reluctant to believe. We also were leary of letting our small town think we're loony. Instead, we sent a unified prayer for this woman's protection.

I've only seen a dark entity twice and have met two people who can see them all the time; they both can actually see light and dark entities both in people and places. In speaking with them, we've found that prayer is the most effective way to dispel the ghosts.

Spirits come in a variety of forms, not all look like humans, but they all are affected by our prayers.

Some typical examples of the non-body presence of a spirit aside from dark or light orbs are doors and windows that open and close on their own, sometime at a specific hour; steps walking down a hallway, across a room or on stairs, or on the roof as in Denver; objects that move or disappear and reappear in strange places- most often keys and photographs. Smells, most frequently smoke but sometimes food or perfume or cologne. The ethereal world sets the stage as to how they'll let you know that they're present and trying to get your attention, or wanting you to leave them alone.

During interviews, I would ask why they thought the entity was a particular gender when it appeared as nonhuman. Again, it's something that those who have experienced the supernatural know. They told me, and all will tell you they don't know how they know, they just do. When spirits materialize the gender is usually obvious. When it's experienced, or felt, you just know what the gender is, unless it's irrelevant or there is a room full of them. That is entirely up to the ghost to disclose.

Chapter 4

HOME MAID

Joan moved into a beautiful country frame house in Copley, Ohio in 1997, which at the time was owned by our brother John. Joan is outrageously funny and incredibly smart. She finds humor in the worst of situations, including her battle with cancer. She's one of the most generous and genuinely kind people I've ever known. I'm glad she's my sister and my dear friend. She married Victor (Vic) Butler in 2008.

The Copley house was built in 1937 by a couple with five children. The two youngest of their children, now elderly, purchased a place just a short walk from their childhood home. I have never discovered what happened to their other three family members, although they told Vic that one had passed away.

John sold the house to Victor when Vic and Joan became engaged; they now live in the Houston area. My son Vincent lived with them briefly on Schocalog Drive in Copley, Ohio.

I have had the pleasure of being a guest in their home on several trips back to the area. On a visit in March 2006 we had finished dinner and were in a conversation about the beautiful landscaping Vic and Joan had done to the property. My mother and niece Chrissy were there also. Vic told us he and Joan had been out in the yard working the week before I arrived when two elderly woman approached him as he worked. They explained that they were sisters, and grew up in the house Vic was now toiling on. They pointed down the street to the house they presently owned and told him that the original one-room house that sat on his lot was currently in their backyard. They explained that their parents lived in the one room house for years until they could afford to build their dream home, which now belonged to Vic.

"You've done a wonderful job with this yard", said the first.

The second nodded in agreement.

"Do you ever go in that room?" As she said this she gave a head gesture and pointed to the second story window, closest to the driveway.

"Sure", replied Vic, and then continued, "We just made a game room for our nephew up there."

Vincent had moved back to the area and was staying with them until he could find a place of his own.

"Well, we were never allowed in that room, but we didn't know why." The second sister explained.

Sister number one chimed in, "We slept in the back bedroom with our two other sisters, mom and dad always kept the baby in their bedroom. That room used to be the baby's room. Mother padlocked it one day and never let us go in there. To this day we don't know why."

The sister continued talking about the old bedroom, what a waste of space it was for them growing up, and later some of the fonder memories that came to mind. After perhaps a half hour of reminiscing, mostly to themselves, they said goodbye to Vic and walked on. They came back later that week with pictures of the way the house used to look, replete with stories for every photo. They were both deceased before I could interview them.

The upstairs has a center hall with the bathroom on the left as you ascend the stairs. Across the hall from the bathroom, although not directly across, is the aforementioned game room which also provides access to the attic. Next to the game room is the master bedroom, across the hall from Vic and Joan's room is the guest bedroom. Victor wakes almost every day at the same time and immediately goes into the bathroom to relieve his bladder. One morning when he was on his way to the bathroom, he saw with his peripheral vision a woman standing in the game room.

He told us after dinner, "At first I thought it was Joanie, then I realized I had just left her in our bedroom, she was asleep."

He said the woman stood facing the wall that divides the room to their bedroom. She looked as though she was "…doing dishes or something with her hands."

Vic described her as a middle-aged woman, white. Her hair is brown and pulled back off her face. She wears a gray dress that hangs to just below the knee. She never looked up at him, but occupies herself with her business of whatever she's doing with her hands. He said this was the second time he'd seen her. Both times were identical, and although she startled him because he never expected to see her, she wasn't frightening. I said, "Vic, I could've sworn you told me you don't believe in ghosts."

He leaned back in his chair, rubbed his belly, and with a huge grin on his face replied, "Well, I've seen this one twice. I'm starting to."

I began to think perhaps the woman wasn't washing dishes, but tending to a baby that passed from sudden infant death syndrome. Maybe this was the caretaker falsely accused of killing an infant, and trying desperately to let us know she is innocent. What the ghost was wearing makes me think she was hired help. Maybe that's why the girls weren't permitted in that bedroom and mom and dad had it padlocked; off limits in their grief. I can only speculate, because all parties involved are now deceased. The woman and the family involved are remembered in our prayers always.

The following occurred at the Schocalog house during my visit home in 2006. We went to Akron to attend my father's funeral Mass.

Traveling with four teenagers can be grueling on a good day, but we had a great road trip in spite of getting lost in Kentucky on the way. (Every time I drive from Dallas to Akron I get lost in Kentucky). Our drive put us in Akron twenty-two hours after we'd left Dallas. It was always wonderful to return to my home town, especially so for my children, who love to visit their brother, cousins, aunts and uncles. Joan and Victor graciously opened their home to us, my son Vincent was staying with them as well. My middle son, Paul, is autistic and epileptic. Although Paul is nonverbal, he manages to get his point across easily to those attempting to listen. Joan and Vic are wonderful with him. We stayed seven days, and had a memorable time.

The first full day was spent at our father's funeral Mass at St. Sebastian Catholic Church; with all a funeral entails for the duration of the day. The next day schedules returned to normal for those who live there.

Joan continued to work, as did Vic and Vince, while we vacationed. The four children and I said our good-byes to all as they left for work, and eventually got on the road to visit my other siblings who lived nearby. Joan was the last to leave at two o'clock in the afternoon. As we stood on her back porch, she took a key from her wallet and put it under the mat saying, "Now you won't have to worry about coming in before someone gets home from work. Come in whenever you want."

I kissed her and she left, second shift meant I wouldn't see her again until close to midnight.

The other four children and I ran all day accompanied by my sister Jane and four of her six kids. We visited Derby Downs where the All-American Soap Box Derby is raced annually, I showed the kids the Goodyear blimp hangar, and took them on a tour of Portage Lakes. We ended our afternoon by stopping for custard at Strickland's, the favorite ice cream stand of locals. Later that evening our plans were to take my mother to dinner and spend the rest of our evening with her. I went back to Joan's house on Schocalog to freshen up and allow the kids to do the same. It was a hot, humid July in Akron, we all felt a bit grungy after being outside most of the day.

The key was right where she'd left it and we hurried in. The house was cooled by a window unit air conditioner located on the first floor; the cool air was a welcome relief.

We were rushing out the backdoor within a half an hour of getting there, when Donald grabbed for the last brownie on the kitchen table. They were in a flimsy plastic container, which he accidentally knocked to the floor in his haste, scattering crumbs in its wake. He hurriedly went to the top of the cellar stairs by the side door and grabbed the broom, and swept the crumbs into a pile while the others were making their way to the car. Donald couldn't find the dustpan, so I told him to leave it and positioned the broom over the pile of brownie crumbs so I would remember to have him finish the job as soon as we got back. I leaned the broom against the washing machine next to the back door, and we left the house. I pulled the key from under the mat, closed and locked the door but decided to keep the key in my pocket. I've heard too many stories of burglars checking under doormats for keys. We were slightly off schedule, but we were on vacation.

When we pulled back into the driveway four hours later, my daughter Genevie exclaimed, "The back door is open, mom. Did you forget to lock it?"

I put the Suburban in park and got out, walked to the front of the truck, turned toward the house and saw that the outer screen door was closed, but the rear entry door was wide open. I know that I locked that door! The kids were filing out of the car, I told them to stay put and started for the house when Donald said in his most chivalrous tone, "You all stay here while I go check it out."

Before I could stop him he disappeared into the house. We were right behind him going in and I saw him as he made the corner onto the stairs from the living room. I told the girls to stay just inside by the back door and keep an eye on their brother Paul; I was going upstairs to make sure Donald was okay and have a peek around myself. The one thing I immediately noticed was that the broom was no longer where I'd left it, propped next to the washer. Donald met me halfway down the stairway and said, "It's all clear, mom. No one's here."

I kissed him, thanking him for being so fearless and said, "I need to use the bathroom, keep your sisters and Paul downstairs, I'll be down in a minute."

I really wanted to inspect the house the way a mom with kids would, under every nook and cranny. When I got to the top of the stairs just outside the bathroom the first thing I noticed was the broom resting against the wall just outside the bathroom door. I went to the top of the stairs and called down to Donald, "Did you bring the broom upstairs when you came up?"

"No ma'am. I didn't touch a thing."

I continued my inspection by entering our guest bedroom next to the bathroom, where Paul and I were sleeping. The drawers on the chest of drawers had been pulled out with such force that socks and boxers had fallen to the floor, some hanging over the edge of the drawer's side. I turned to my right, facing the closet, the door was wide open and all the clothes had been pushed to one side, as though someone could have been hiding in it. I dashed to the window at the back of the room. It overlooks the backyard and I wondered if it were possible that an intruder could've jumped out the window when he heard us come in. The window was locked, not a bit of dust removed from the window sill. (It's almost impossible to find dust anywhere in Joan's house, anyway- she's meticulous.) I got on the floor and checked under the bed. Empty.

 I had a feeling as I was putting everything in its proper place that I shouldn't be doing that. What if the police had to be called? I'd just altered a crime scene. What really bothered me was that I don't know why that thought kept coming into my head. I also had a sinking, gnawing feeling in my stomach. Something was wrong, but I couldn't say what it was. I felt powerless to protect my children, even though I was doing all I could to do just that.

 The children had already filed into the house, making themselves at home in the living room, parked in front of the television. I was restless and decided to brush down the carpeted stairway, since the broom had to be taken downstairs, anyway. I often clean to relieve frustration and think things through. I finished the stairs and continued into the living room, which has wooden flooring. I received only a few grunts as I momentarily blocked my kid's view of the television, before going into the kitchen to continue sweeping. I had just begun the kitchen when Paul came from the living room with a bottle of bubbles, motioning to me that he wanted to blow them. I directed him to the basement since it was dark outside, and he gleefully was on his way downstairs to blow soap all over the concrete basement floor. Donald arrived within seconds of Paul descending the stairs and followed behind, exclaiming as he went, "Basements are so cool, I wish we had one!"

 Of course, there are very few basements in Texas.

 I thought about the way the drawers in Vince's room had been pulled out, the clothing in the closet being pushed to one side, and the broom upstairs. He must've gotten off work early and had a date or something. That would explain everything, so mystery solved!

 I left the kitchen long enough to put a blanket over the girls, who had fallen asleep on the floor in front of the television. I was back in the kitchen sweeping when Vince walked in the back

door. I stopped what I was doing to kiss him hello. "How'd your date go tonight, honey?"

"I didn't have a date. I've been at work since the last time I saw you."

I explained what we saw when we came in the house, and we both agreed that perhaps the neighbor kids had come into the house. I'd completely forgotten until later as I was getting ready for bed and found the house key in my pocket that the neighbors couldn't have taken the key from under the mat, I had it on me the entire time.

Joan followed Vince home from work by perhaps twenty minutes. I didn't want to tell her about the incident, she looked tired and didn't need any more emotional strain. Vince argued that it was her house, and that she had a right to know, especially since it was a possible intrusion. I agreed and he went into the living room, sat on the couch next to his aunt, and spoke quietly with her. She'd gone to the living room to visit with my daughters, relax and enjoy a cigarette after a long day. Vince went upstairs to shower, I heard him running up the stairs.

Simultaneously, I felt three successive thumps under my feet as I stood in the kitchen, as though someone had taken a broom handle or other heavy object and thrust it against the ceiling in the basement. "Donald," I yelled, "you can stop now!"

"Stop what?" His reply came from the doorway leading down to the basement, just a few feet behind me.

He said, "Mom, I heard those thumps as I came up the stairs, and thought you were trying to freak me out by pounding the broom handle on the floor. I saw the dust falling from the ceiling as I walked up the stairs."

We were both speechless, staring into each other's faces as if we didn't believe what the other was saying. Paul immediately came running up from the basement and began pulling on my arm in the direction of the basement stairwell. He is nonverbal, but some words he says distinctly. He kept repeating, "Ghost, two ghost!"

Paul's word sounded more like 'goat', but both Donald and I knew what he was saying. He had a look of torment in his eyes, just short of terror. He was adamant about my looking into the basement, pulling me forcibly in that direction. My sister heard all this and came to join our trio at the top of the stairs. Paul put his hands up to his face as if playing peek-a-boo and said, "Boo, two ghosts!"

He was pointing down into the basement, then held up two fingers, and repeated "ghosts" several more times. He would only let go of my arm long enough to gesture, then hold it again. He was holding onto my arm (which he does whenever he's uncertain or frightened) so tightly he left bruises. I'd never seen Paul like this before. I wanted not to believe it, so I told him to go back downstairs to blow his bubbles. He pushed me out of the way, saying, "Na na na na na …" as he went into the living room; in Paul speak, that means no. He was shaking his head violently from side to side as he said this, and he looked frightened, one of only a few times I've seen him scared. After no more than a minute alone in the living room Paul joined us again in the kitchen and took my left arm, although not as tightly this time. He pointed to the t-shirt Joan had put on after work and repeated several times "Ghost, two ghost", and again pointed in the direction of the basement. (Joan was wearing a 'dead-head' t-shirt with a skeleton on it.)

Joanie, seeing her nephew so adamant and frightened, immediately went into combat mode. "Aw, hell no you don't…where's my holy water?"

Those who know Joan know she rarely uses profanity. She grabbed her Holy water bottle from the hall table on her way down the stairs, stating loudly as she descended for 'her' to get out of her house "...in God's name get out..." as she splashed holy water around the basement.

We all stood at the top of the stairs dumbfounded, waiting until she came back up, perhaps a minute later. She slammed the empty water bottle back on the table and walked over to hug Paul. "That should knock her ass out. I've already got five people staying here, I don't need any more!" She let out her bodacious laugh, and it calmed us all.

Joan doesn't know why she addressed the entity as feminine, except that Vic had seen the ghost of a woman at the house. She said she just 'thought' it was female, even though she saw nothing in the basement.

Joan and Victor both told me that strange noises and events

continued to occur on a regular basis after that; the typical stuff like car keys missing, objects moved from one location to another, and water running. Because there were three people living there I would attribute these happenings to forgetfulness, although they would disagree. I don't want to put anything on these pages that can be dispelled by scientific reasoning. Some events could be attributed to human error; but the broom being upstairs when I left it downstairs, the pounding on the floor or the ceiling, etc. I was there and was personally affected. Feelings cannot be created, feelings just are.

What Paul saw, experienced and said was the most compelling evidence I have. Everyone that was there and saw him that night agrees with me, and no one knows Paul better than myself, his siblings and his aunt.

I've also been told by several people that those with mental handicaps similar to Paul's autism re much more likely to be recipients of ethereal phenomenon. I know that Paul has had several 'conversations' when there have been no human beings in the room. I've always assumed it's because Paul can't communicate like the rest of his family, but I've also learned not to discount the supernatural entirely. I know the entities at my sister's house scared Paul tremendously. He wanted no part of them and wanted his mom to get rid of them. His Godmother did that for me, thanks Joanie!

Chapter 5

COPLEY KELPIE

Cecilia (Celia) is the seventh in our large family- she'll also be the first to tell you she's the favorite. She was painfully shy as an infant and young girl. Our parents later discovered it was because she was highly intelligent, wanting to absorb the world around her like a sponge. She's still relatively quiet at first, but when she speaks, it's authoritative and smart. She's a fantastic business woman, wife and mother.

She and Dan purchased their dream home on about an acre of land in Copley, Ohio shortly after they were married. It was a spectacular and spacious center stair colonial. It was also vacant and in much need of the TLC that only a starry-eyed newlywed couple could give it. I don't mean that either are unrealistic; quite the opposite would be true of both, they are very pragmatic. The thought of taking on such a huge property overhaul scared every other buyer away, though. Not Celia and Dan, they jumped in with both feet! They were high school sweethearts and have been together for over forty years, and have five beautiful, intelligent offspring. They are two of the best parents I've ever known. They have also traveled extensively, seeing many parts of the country and world. In all of her travels, she never experienced anything remotely close to what happened at their 'dream home'.

This is the exact story sent from Cecilia to me. I changed only the font, as the script she originally used was difficult to read:

My first recollection of any spiritual activity at my home was shortly after we had moved

into the home. I am a fanatic about keeping my kitchen cabinets closed and I would enter the room and find most, if not all, the cabinet doors open. At the time I didn't think anything of it because I had experienced the earthquake in Akron in 1986 and was aware that there were tremors through the area that weren't always felt by an average person going about their daily activities. This went on for quite some time without me realizing what was actually happening. The spirit, not wanting to be ignored, made herself known one day with a bang! I was playing with my infant daughter, Megan, in our living room when all of the sudden a loud clatter came from the upstairs! I grabbed my daughter, the cordless phone and my car keys and ran out the door. I pulled my car to the bottom of my driveway, where I could watch both exits of the house but have enough of a head start in case someone came out of the house after me. I called my brother, John knowing that he was in the area. I never like to call the police unless I feel that I am in danger.

John showed up with a friend of his and they searched my house with their weapon of choice, the baseball bat! The only thing they found in the house was that everything in my bathroom was in my bathtub, as if it all fell in at once. Again I assumed that there was another tremor that I was unable to feel.

These sorts of things went on for years with me explaining them away as another tremor, or that I was simply forgetting to close the cabinet. I'm sure that I wasn't accepting these extraordinary happenings as a haunting because my husband, Dan, was traveling quite a bit at the time and I didn't want to be the only adult left in a haunted house!

There came a day when I did call the police. It was one of the times Dan was out of town. He was due home the next day. It was early October and had been warm during the day, but was starting to freeze that night. I was just putting Megan to bed and as I bent down to pick up her humidifier to fill, a loud BANG pounded on the window that was right at my head. I looked out the window to see if a neighborhood kid was out in the yard throwing apples or anything else at the house. I didn't see anyone. I was shaken, but stayed calm so that Megan wouldn't get uptight. As I returned to her room to put the humidifier back down two more BANGS hit the window! At this point I hit the floor! I crawled across the room and took Megan out of her crib. I went to my room, grabbed the phone and called my brothers! Neither one was home but my mom said she would contact them and send one over. I hung up with her and called the police! They came out and searched around the house. He couldn't find anything out of place and there weren't rocks or anything else under the window that, if thrown, would have made such an incredibly loud noise. The officer did say that there were cats out there and that maybe a cat had climbed the tree nearby (the tree/bush didn't go anywhere near the height of the window) and maybe it hit the window. I told him, "Sir, with all due respect, the only way a cat could have made that noise is if someone picked it up and threw it at my house!"

He asked if I wanted him to search the house, which I declined. I knew there wasn't anyone in the house. I wasn't afraid at this point, just a bit confused. My brother, Greg, came over to stay with me for the rest of the night! He wasn't too happy to be there until I handed him the remote control and a beer and told him there was more in the fridge! The rest of the night was quiet.

Another encounter was when I was pregnant with my second child, Katie. Again, Dan was out of town and due home the next day. He had been gone for two weeks without any occurrence, or one that I was willing to acknowledge. For some reason I was a little spooked that evening and asked my brother, John to come stay with me. We stayed up talking and watching TV. I went to bed about 11:00, a bit later that my usual time. At about midnight I heard a loud banging from the living room, which is beneath my bedroom. I thought it was John trying to open the hide-a-bed. I put a pillow over my head and went back to sleep. I was awakened again at 3:00AM with the same noise. This time I went downstairs to see what the problem was. John was sound asleep on the couch. He didn't open the hide-a-bed. The house was very quiet. I went back to bed only to be awakened again at 6:00AM with the same noise! At breakfast the next morning, around 8:00AM, I asked John what in the world he was doing that was keeping me up all night! He stopped eating his breakfast mid spoonful and said "I thought that was you! I thought that you were having some crazy pregnant woman nesting episode and felt like cleaning out your drawers and banging them shut!" He thought the noise was coming from above him and I thought the noise was coming from below me! We went outside to see if something happened to the side of the house and there was nothing wrong. We learned that one of the neighbor's houses had been robbed that night. If the robbers would have made that much noise they would have been caught in the act. Was it the spirit trying to awaken us to stop the robbers? We don't know, we never will. John never stayed with me again!

. Things remained peaceful until Dan had gone on an extended business trip to Korea. He was gone again for two weeks. Everything was fine until the night before he was to come home. I had put the kids to bed and had stayed up for a little bit to do some reading. I then brushed my teeth and as I was leaving the bathroom I heard some cabinets shut. I couldn't tell if they were behind me or the cabinets downstairs in the kitchen. I know this sounds strange, but the noise wasn't loud, it almost seemed to echo. I went down to check the kitchen and everything was in place. I checked and made sure that all of the windows and doors were locked. I searched the basement and found that to be secure as well. At this point I wasn't scared, just confused. I went to bed. About five minutes later, just as I was about to fall asleep, I heard a loud crashing sound! It sounded as if a shelf in a closet had fallen. I got up, grabbed the cordless phone from my nightstand, and as I did I heard an even louder crash! I opened the closet in the hallway, which was right outside my bedroom, and everything was in order. I ran to my daughter's room and grabbed her out of bed and ran to the nursery. I called the police this time. They were at my front door within minutes! I was too terrified to leave the room and go down the stairs to let them in. The dispatcher told me that they could break down the front door if I wanted them too! I didn't want to deal with replacing a broken door so I mustered up enough courage and ran to the door to let them in. There must have been ten police officers that searched my entire house, including my attic! They found nothing had been disturbed. They couldn't find anything that had fallen over that would have made that kind of clatter! I felt very foolish but very relieved at the same time. I didn't sleep well that night.

Again, everything remained quiet for awhile. A noise here and a bang there were always readily explained away as "the kids playing." One recurring experience had me a bit concerned. It wasn't happening to me, but rather to my oldest daughter, Megan.
Whenever she would wake from her nap she would either run down the stairs and hug me as if she had been frightened or she would scream at the top of her lungs from her bedroom. This went on for a few weeks when she finally told me that every time she would wake up there would be a lady at the bottom of her bed. I let her nap in my room, thinking that a change of scenery would be good for her. This didn't work. One day after she had awakened frightened I asked her to describe the woman and she said that she looked like me "except she had a beak-like mouth." At this point I didn't let her watch "Duck Tales" the cartoon anymore. I thought that there might be something about the cartoon that scared her. Things were calm for a week or so, until one morning in August of 1990 when I couldn't explain a series of very strange happenings. Megan was sleeping later than usual that morning and I was up with Katie. I was reading a book to her in the playroom when a cylinder shaped toy took one revolution toward us and stopped! The toy usually made noise when it rolled but this time it was eerily quiet! We got

up and walked out of the room. I didn't want to react too much to it because I didn't want to let Katie know that it really scared me. We went upstairs to wake Megan, so that I could get the girls dressed and leave the house for the day. I made pancakes for breakfast for the girls that morning. I can still smell the syrup that they got all over themselves, including their hair! As I cleared the table I told them to go upstairs and get ready for a bath. As I rinsed the dishes I heard what sounded like my girls falling down the stairs. I ran over to see what it was and it was Megan and Katie standing there looking as if they were just electrocuted or had just seen a ghost! They had not fallen down the stairs, but had run down! I was afraid that they may have been shocked by my hair dryer which was in the bathroom by the sink. Megan had just turned 3 and Katie was a little over a year.

Running down the steps is not something that is mastered until a child is a bit bigger and older, unless of course they have seen a ghost, which in this case is what had happened! I ran over and hugged them and asked them what was wrong. Megan looked up at me, and through a much shaken voice said just one word, "ghost!" I didn't understand how a child would know what a ghost was or where she would have heard the term. I sat down with the girls on my lap and asked them to tell me what happened. Megan started to tell me what the "lady" had said to them in a deep, scratchy voice. When I heard her talk like this, the hair on my arms and the back of my neck stood on end. She said that they heard a noise in my bedroom and when they went in they saw this "lady ghost" in my closet. She couldn't understand what was being said to her, but they knew that this lady wanted them to get into the closet with her and her children that she had with her. I told Megan that if she ever saw this lady again she was to tell her that she was not allowed to talk to strangers and that I wanted to see and talk with her. Megan responded, "No Mommy, she's too scary."

This broke my heart because I knew how terrified Megan must have been. This made me instantly angry with this "entity." At this point I told the girls that I was going upstairs to see for myself. They both held onto me and buried their faces in my shoulders and begged me not to go up there. I told them, "This is our home and we are not going to be afraid." I was raised to believe that if you have been baptized and believe that God is your protector, then a ghost can't harm you. This must be where my strength came from, because I am a devout chicken.

As I made it to my bedroom door, with two terrified girls strangling me, I saw that my door had been slammed shut. I couldn't just turn the knob and go in, the door was jammed. I asked the girls who shut he door and Megan said she did! I had to put them down and slam into it with my shoulder a few times in order to open it. As I approached my closet my girls hid their faces and started to cry. When I showed them that the closet was empty and asked them where "the lady" was they both pointed to the same spot. They never agree on anything, but they did that day. I quickly bathed them and called my mom. I asked her if she had holy water, or if she could get some from her church. She didn't ask any questions and came right over. When she got to my house she could tell that I was unnerved. I told her that the girls had seen something, but didn't tell her what or where. I told her that I was leaving and that I would meet her at her house later. She went through the house and blessed it as she said, "In the name of Jesus Christ be gone!"

How she knew what to say, I don't know she didn't know either. She said she either read it somewhere or saw it in a movie. She said that saying it seemed to give her strength and kept her calm. This is not something that my mom usually does, but she is a very religious person. She seemed like the best candidate for the job at the time! She told me later that as she entered my bedroom and approached the closet she got goose bumps all over her body and the hair on her arms stood up! She said she was overcome with anger and started yelling, "How dare you frighten my daughter and grandchildren. You get out!"

This episode has earned my mom the nickname, "Dr. Vinkman" from the movie "Ghost Busters!"

Things were quiet and calm for years! Dan would travel and I would be fine in the house alone. We had more children without incidents at nap time. I moved the playroom to the basement and the kids loved to go down there and play. It was a big room with nothing but toys, and they had a great time. I loved it too because my living room was easier to keep clean.

We lived and entertained in the home for years. Nothing out of the ordinary happened while Dan was home or away. The nights before he was to come home from a business trip were now as uneventful as any other. We had our fourth child and felt that the house was getting to be too small for us. It had three bedrooms, one being the size of a small nursery. We thought that we could add onto the house or find a bigger one. We chose to find a bigger one in a neighborhood that had city water. I was working as a real estate agent at the time and put the house on the market with my broker. This is when things started to happen again!

At first the things that were happening could be explained as just dumb luck. For instance, our basement was now getting very wet in one corner, with standing water.

Our basement had been bone dry for the entire ten years that we lived there. We fixed the downspout and it seemed to fix the problem for the time being. We had a heavy rain and the corner stayed dry, so we thought we had fixed the problem. I had a showing on a day that was raining off and on, mostly off. The corner was very wet that day. The buyer was not interested in the house because she had had numerous problems before with wet basements and didn't want to deal with the problem of potential mold. The corner was dry that evening!

One morning a few days later, as I was getting my daughters ready for school I noticed my four year old son, Danny, playing with naked, headless Barbie dolls! I asked what happened to the doll's heads and was informed that my nephew had torn them off the day before when he was over for a party. I was also informed that another nephew, Johnny, had educated my son about the female anatomy!

Danny said to me, "I know what these are," as he ran his thumbs over the plastic Barbie breasts."
I said, "Oh really what are they?" Expecting anything other than what I heard.
He replied, "They're called boobs! Johnny told me!"
I informed my son of the proper terminology and took the Barbie dolls from him. I then told him to go find some trucks to play with. I threw the headless Barbie dolls down the basement steps so that I could put them back into the playroom, and maybe find the heads to them. After the girls left for school I gathered all of the dirty laundry. I informed the boys that I would be in the basement doing laundry, but that I would be back upstairs soon. I didn't want them in the basement that morning because it was chilly in the playroom and they were still in their pajamas. As I carried the basket of clothing down to the basement I was careful to close the door behind me all the way. I was overly cautious because my youngest son had fallen down the basement stairs and suffered a fractured skull. As I walked down the stairs I kicked the Barbie dolls down the stairs and into the playroom. The washing machine and dryer were on the opposite side of the basement from the playroom. At the time we had well water and our well took a long time to fill the washing machine. As the machine filled with water I sorted laundry. After being down there for a few minutes I heard a loud bang on the steps. I was terrified that my youngest had opened the door and would attempt the stairs again. I yelled for them to close the door as I shoved the clothes into the washing machine. I ran to the steps and found that the door was still closed all the way and the Barbie dolls had returned to the steps! My blood ran cold! I was so scared I couldn't move for a moment.

Then I thought of my little boys upstairs by themselves and picked up the dolls and threw them back into the playroom! I ran up those stairs faster than I had ever run before or since! I was shaking for the rest of the day. Later that afternoon, as my youngest took his nap and the others played outside I called my mom, a.k.a.Dr. Vinkman, and told her what had happened in the basement that morning. As I was telling her this, the glass doors on my fireplace front opened and closed right in front of my eyes! My mom said that our ghost friend didn't want us to leave! We were leaving anyway!

We had unusual things happen in the house even as it was being shown to prospective buyers. There was one couple who heard a strange scratching noise and turned to the real estate agent and asked, "Is this house haunted? This is the same noise that I hear at my apartment and my apartment is haunted." The agent didn't know what to say because she didn't hear anything!

Even the couple that eventually bought the house had a few unexplainable experiences as they looked at the house. Before they wrote an offer they wanted their parents to look at the house. As they were about to leave they heard a strange noise. The buyer said, "Oh I bet that's Dad outside just trying to scare us." And her mother turned to the house, and not talking to anyone in particular said, "Oh Casper, just leave us alone!" When they got to the door, which had been less than ten feet from them they saw that her dad was waiting in the car, and couldn't have made the noise on the opposite side of the house!

When this same couple had a home inspection, one of the inspectors called them into the bathroom, and informed them that they were going to have a problem with water pressure. This was something that we had learned to live with. We had informed the buyers that you couldn't wash clothes and take a shower at the same time, but this man seemed to think that the problem was bigger than that. He had us all go to the bathroom for his demonstration. He turned on the shower, then turned the water on in the sink and then flushed the toilet. There was no change in water pressure! The inspector was baffled! He said that he had just done the same test before we were in the room and that there was no pressure! The buyers felt that maybe the holding tank had been filling up

when he had checked it before and didn't feel that the water pressure was going to be an issue. This had never happened in my home before! If someone flushed the toilet while you were in the shower, you were usually left with little or no water.

These buyers proceeded with the purchase of the home. As I was going through the home on my final walk through I came around the corner from the dining room to go up the stairs. As I took my first step up I looked and there at the top of the steps was "the lady!" She was wearing a peach colored dress with off white lacing, June Cleaver style. She disappeared just as quickly as she had appeared. I didn't go upstairs. I left everything that was up there and left the house. I never went back.

We were happy in our new home when the buyers bought and took possession of our old home. A few months after they had settled in, the buyer, who was also a friend of my sister's, asked my sister if I had ever said anything about the house being haunted!

Our sister, Cathy, was approached by the woman at a local grocery store several months after purchasing the house. After a few minutes of polite conversation, the woman asked, "Did your sister ever have weird things happen at her house?" Cathy didn't know how to respond, so she asked as she put her hand on her heart, "What on Earth do you mean?"

Cathy told me she didn't want to tell the woman, "Oh yeah, the ghost is why she moved!"

The lady said nothing, fearing she'd be thought a fool, like so many others I've spoken with regarding ghosts. I hope she buys the book.

Celia and Dan's house was built in 1956. At the time, Copley was an agricultural town, with various sized farms scattered throughout the area. From the description Celia gave of the clothing worn by the female ghost living in their home, "June Cleaver style", I believe it was the original owner. She and her husband had built a massive center-stair Colonial on an acre of land; no one was good enough to live in her house. She'd make sure of that by scaring them away.

Chapter 6

LITTLE BOY BLUE

One day while my children and I were staying with Joan and Vic in 2006, we visited Celia and Dan in their new home for an informal gathering of family and family friends. The weather was typical of Ohio summers; hot and always a possibility of rain. It rained this particular July day.

My daughter Elizabeth climbed to the top of a step-stool in Celia's kitchen, which gave her a full view of the back yard, to watch the other family members scramble when an unexpected rain shower popped up. She laughed as she looked out the double-paned glass over the kitchen sink. Her aunts and uncles, cousins and friends running for cover as the rain intensified.

We'd all finally taken cover indoors and the rain continued to pelt their house when Elizabeth came to me and said, "Mom, there was a little boy standing at the bottom of the ladder a few minutes ago."

"Well honey, there are a lot of little boys here, which one?" I asked.

"None here." She stated flatly.

I didn't understand at the time, partially because of the excitement of being with my family; from the trauma of my father's death, and I'm sure partly because of the overwhelming festivities of the day.

Elizabeth and I talked later on the long drive home to Dallas. She told me about a young boy, perhaps 6 or 7, in a striped shirt and shorts standing at the bottom of the ladder that day in the kitchen. He was the same boy Celia's daughter had seen in her new house; upstairs in the master bath just inside the closet.

When I called my sister after returning to Dallas the next day, Celia didn't want to discuss it.

She'd had enough of ghosts from her last house and her children had sustained enough traumas. Any talk of the supernatural was strictly prohibited in or around her family. She did confide to me in that phone conversation that her youngest, Alaina, had seen this little boy standing in the doorway of the master closet.

Celia was in the bathroom getting ready for work. She placed Alaina on the vanity in front of her to keep her close, and Alaina told her mother the little boy was standing behind her in the doorway of the closet. Celia saw nothing in the mirror, so she turned around to see no one in the bathroom or the closet. She knew from experience that spirits appeared to her children so she told Alaina, "Tell the little boy to go be with God."

Alaina leaned to the left of her mother, and said, "My mom says you need to go be with God now."

Celia said she watched her daughter's expression change from quizzical to happy. Then she looked her mother in the eyes, shrugged her shoulders and matter-of-factly said, "He's gone now."

Elizabeth went on to describe that as she watched the family in the back yard run for cover, she wanted to get down from the ladder and tease her cousins for getting caught in the rain. As she turned to descend the ladder, this young boy was standing at its base, obstructing her passing, just staring at her.

She told me that she immediately knew it was a ghost, but felt compelled to respond. (This was repeated by several people about their interaction with ghosts.) She asked him what he wanted, and was answered with a blank stare. He evidently just wanted to be with our family- never responding but eventually dissipating into thin air to allow her to leave her perch on the ladder. She told me that she felt as though he wanted more, yet felt no malice or ill-intent from him. Again- she felt it, no words were spoken, no gestures made. Elizabeth knew the boy had come to be a part of our family for whatever reason. We will never know why. I believe my daughter. I trust this entity showed himself to her and my niece because he saw something he wanted to be a connected with.

As far as I know, there have been no further sightings of the boy since we were in Ohio that summer. I won't ever try to research him or why he showed himself, but we prayed for him as a family and individually that he went to be with God.

Trying to find the reasons ghost appear is as futile as trying to grasp them.
I've spent thousands of hours in exhaustive research to no avail. I've found spirits can be as elusive in history as they can be in the present.

Chapter 7

SENSORY OVERLOAD

I have read and researched several books prior to writing this one. There are some explanations for what's happened in the previous pages perhaps, but none are scientific. Ghost hunters and those of us interested in people who have preceded us in death have a story to tell- we try to make sense of things that have no sense, but that doesn't make them any less real.

That is the dilemma I face. The stories are true, there is no research per se' in ghosts; it's all subject to speculation, regardless of what 'experts' have to say. I also know there are gifted people in this world that can see and communicate with spirits. The television show 'Ghost Whisperer' was based on such a person. I have personally seen light and dark entities, and the ghost of Bacon (I didn't realize at the time that I was seeing a ghost, I thought it was a person) so I know they exist, but I don't consider myself an expert on the subject. The only group I would consider expert in the field of the paranormal would be exorcists. Theirs is a very dangerous line of work because they actually become a 'hostage of the devil' to salvage souls. If you pray, you pray to spirits so you believe ghosts exist, too.

Allow me to play devil's advocate, (pardon the pun).The senses involved were:

Sight: What was seen was seen- first person accounts. They were viewed with eyes that properly function, on people of all ages that use them every day in the 'real' world. Those that saw some ghosts actually thought they were seeing a live person, even though subconsciously they knew it couldn't have been a live person. Apparitions appeared both in daytime and night. I've spoken with those who've seen orbs, or faint whispers of ghost-like whitish-blue light. Their vision was fine as well. The majority of people who see ghosts rub their eyes almost immediately, as though their eyes are deceiving them.

Smell: Some involved the smell of smoke, as in Dee's case; a rancor odor or musty smell often preceded the Burton ghost. Many Marian apparitions include a strong scent of roses; which is why the Mother of God is often referred to as 'Our Lady of the Rose' by Catholics. I was thinking of my uncle Ivan while driving home from work one summer evening and smelled the cologne he wore almost daily, 'Old Spice', even though the air conditioner was running and all my windows were rolled up. My mother once told me she smelled Noxzema skin cream, which her mom used daily. She was standing at the kitchen sink, thinking of her mother on Mother's Day.

The olfactory sense is very powerful, whether the smell is delightful or horrid, it definitely can jog one's memory.

Hearing: Everyone who told these tales heard something. A bell or wind chime, steps, voices, music or a melody in their heads. Often the ghosts 'said' things. These voices were heard inside the head, however, not as an outside reverberation of the eardrum. There are exceptions. For example, a poltergeist rolling a ball, as happened at Celia's; knocking on doors and windows, or as with Dolores and I in Colorado, a crescendo of voices; not one discernible; but when it came to individuals receiving a message from a spirit, they were always heard 'inside' the head of the recipient. The spiritual world uses the mind to communicate with the world of the living, either telepathically or in dreams.

Touch: Feeling chilled was the most common, even during the warmest of days. In the extreme, welts on my niece Celia's back. A mattress compressing in an area as though someone were sitting on it, with no one there; doors unable to be opened as usual with no apparent reason, my computer locking, not allowing access to folders or emails; static on phone lines, sometimes resulting in a small electrical shock. Others have told me stories of being tripped or pushed, especially down stairs. Other instances are cars that won't start for any apparent mechanical reason, or appliances that go on the fritz, sometimes giving a slight electrical shock as well. Although rare, some entities have the ability to touch you, or to throw objects at you with the intent of doing harm. The breeze at my cousin Kathy's

house was so strong it blew her sister's hair into their faces.
Taste: Occasionally people will have a sweet or bitter taste in their mouth when encountering a spirit, either before or after an occurrence. Most often the correlation isn't made until I ask if they've had a sensation in their tongue. The tongue is very sensitive to stimuli- being the largest organ in the head. Taste is crucial because it's not a sense usually thought of when encountering spirits. It was only after all other senses were recognized that people realized the sense of taste was used as a separate vehicle to let us know spirits were present.

Let me give you an example: You're mourning your father who has been gone for x number of years. Sitting in your apartment alone, you wish you could be eating an ice-cream sundae with your father, something you would do together every Sunday while he was living. You taste the sundae as you imagine this. Psychiatrists will tell you that your mind is functioning properly. True, but I am here to tell you that your father wants to have a sundae with you just as badly as you want to have one with him, and you can taste the ice cream your father is sharing with you.

Someone offered a similar story when she found out about my book. This woman tasted strawberries; her sister's favorite snack. She mourned her sister's death daily, remembering how much she loved strawberries. As thoughts of memories with her sister flooded back to her, she could taste strawberries, even though she hadn't eaten them for months.
 It wasn't until hours later that she realized that her sister had been murdered on that day twelve years prior. Perhaps her sister was reminding her to pray for her soul.
 There is no way in the here-and-now to overcome the bridges that divide our worlds; Christ promised He would. Until then, I think we should roll with what the other side has to offer us; to listen to their messages, and to 'pray unceasingly' for their souls, as Christ Himself asked of us.

This brings me to the last sense, which many of you don't think exists, but often use subconsciously:

Sensation: the sixth sense. This is the sense most used when encountering the supernatural, but most expelled when discussing what was seen, heard, tasted or otherwise experienced by the rational senses. Ghosts, spirits and poltergeists are sensed before they're seen most of the time.

In every case I asked what the person 'felt' prior to their particular encounter. Dave was tired, off work and thinking of nothing but going to bed. He was conscientious about waking his kids and wife, but not so anxious that he would conjure an image in his head. Every person asked said they felt 'something', most commonly expressed as anxiety. This is not to say they made images appear. I'll reiterate- no one wanted to see what they saw. They were not in control.

Not all entities were the crepuscular variety either, although the majority happened during twilight or nighttime. The little boy at Celia's, the nanny at Joan's and the young man who assisted me at the title bureau are a few of the 'daytime' ghosts. Again, they decide when to appear.

Dreams are the most significant and practical way the spiritual world will communicate with us humans. There are numerous instances of dreams in the Bible, the Torah and the Koran. I knew my aunt Dolores had died hours before I got the call from my mother. She came to me in a dream to say goodbye. I woke up crying because I knew she was gone, which I knew for a certainty when I saw my mother's number on caller ID two hours later. Mom confirmed her death, and felt consoled that her sister came to say goodbye to me.

I had another dream years afterward; a friend of mine couldn't find some legal papers he desperately needed to sell his house. He asked if I'd go through his file cabinets to see if 'fresh eyes' might locate them. Both he and his deceased wife had businesses, with all the mountains of federal and state paperwork required to run a business; four five-drawer file cabinets full. His deceased wife came to me in a dream the same day he asked for my help and told me that she put the papers he was looking for in his medical files. She was one of my dearest friends and I was helping her husband because she was no longer here and able to help him herself. I woke from my nap and immediately went to his medical file. There they were, just as she told me. She knew he would look in his medical files eventually, which is why she didn't put them with the other papers regarding the house.

"He'll go to the doctor before he sells the house." She laughingly told me in the dream.

He could not believe they were there, he'd looked everywhere except his medical files!

Chapter 8

HIPPY HERE

Cathy is my youngest sister. She has had no sightings except for the two below, when she was at the Burton home. The following is the direct e-mail I received from her:

Flag this message

Ghost Stories

Thursday, September 21, 2006 10:11 AM

From:

" Cathy"

Add sender to Contacts

To:

"Susan Taylor (E-mail)" <smtaylorart@yahoo.com>

Good morning,

I decided to email you from work since I realize I will never be able to do so from home.
Story 1: I was babysitting in the upstairs apartment. It was late but I was wide awake watching hockey (it was a short-lived fanatical passion.)
Out of nowhere, a woman walked passed the doorway, which was at 1 o'clock to me--nearly directly in front of me, plainly visible. At first I was just pissed and yelled, "What the hell Beth, why didn't you say hi or somethin?" She

didn't answer me so I followed her into the kitchen. It then occurred to me that this woman had long brown hair--nearly to her butt and was wearing a floppy hat. The hat was crazy out of style and Beth had recently cut her hair a la Rod Stewart, "If you think I'm sexy..." Realizing it was not my sister, I now wondered where this "person" went, so I ran to my niece Nikki's room to make sure she was OK. She was sleeping soundly. It then occurred to me that this "person" could not have gotten passed me. I had gotten up immediately and followed her to the kitchen. There was no way out but passed me. It was then it occurred to me, "I do believe in spooks, I do, I do, I do!" I called Mom. She calmed me down--telling me to state loudly, "get thee gone, Satan." Of course I didn't, but she also offered to come up with holy water, which I believe she did several times to no avail.

Story 2: Being a glutton for punishment, about 4 years later, I moved into said haunted apartment. I had forgotten the incident--I babysat many times thereafter and never saw a thing. After a couple months, I began to be awakened by someone walking heavily up and down the stairwell, just outside my bedroom door. Though Nikki was directly across the hall from me, she never heard a thing. It sounded as if someone was running full force on those old oak steps then pacing just outside my door. It was terrifying. I lost a lot of sleep--it would occur 3-4 times a week. I got frustrated and would run out to confront him/her but find no one there. I started to call out, "show yourself or go away," then, "show yourself or go to hell," then "show yourself or F*** Off!!" None of that worked either--they were never to be seen, merely heard. I finally accepted the fact that they were going to torment me regularly and started to pray the rosary instead of "cursing the darkness." My rosary, (until I swept it up accidentally a few months ago) was always hanging on my bedpost. I would wear it to sleep nightly and wake up with funky marks about my neck. Without them though, I never would've gotten rest for the years I lived there.

There you have it. It's my story and I'm sticking to it!

Thank You,

Cathy Lillis

Compliance Specialist

 The irony is that Cathy gave little credit to the powers of the sacramental: (holy water, blessed rosaries, etc.) until she was at her wits end, because the blessed Rosary around her neck is what kept the evil at bay. Her humor is contagious, and that's how she dealt with the ghosts, which you will find is a common theme with the entire family.
 The house she's referring to is the Burton house where Dave saw the female apparition and my son Vince and others saw the male who told Vince his name was Bacon. The instance where Cathy only heard the footsteps could have been the ghost of Bacon's daughter, who was always seen in the rear of the house near the stairwell and hall. I believe that is where she was when she died.
 I believe the ghost Cathy saw, the one with the floppy hat and long brown hair, is the ghost of the previous homeowner's daughter. I was told they had a teenaged daughter who died of a drug overdose, but there were no family members alive to question about her death by the time I began to research this book. A death or suicide in the house was never disclosed when I purchased Burton in 1984, as is required by law now. The female 'hippy' with the floppy hat was only seen that one time by my sister.

 My sister Dolores currently lives in that apartment. She was taking the trash cans to the curb the night prior to the cities designated trash pick-up day. It was a beautiful August evening in 2017.
 The neighbor, who had recently purchased the house next door said hello, as she was on her way to the curb with her trash cans

as well. They introduced each other, and after brief pleasantries the new neighbor asked Dee, "I don't want you to think I'm crazy, but did the previous owner ever talk about ghosts' in this house?" As she pointed to her own.

My sister laughed and answered, "No, but we've had quite a few of them in ours. I don't consider you crazy at all."

The woman went on to explain that she saw what she thought was an intruder standing in her kitchen as she went in to make coffee one morning. She asked the girl in the floppy hat with long brown hair, "What are you doing here?"

She became concerned when she got no response that the girl was probably on drugs, and had broken in to burglarize her home, possibly to harm her as well. Then the girl vanished. It's then that this new homeowner realized it was an apparition. She told Dee that was the only time she'd seen the girl in the floppy hat, but it was a frightening experience for her. She went on to tell Dee that she also saw the ghost of a woman wearing a long white nightgown in the center stairwell of the house, leading to the second floor. This entity didn't interact with her at all, either, but seemed sad as she ascended the stairs. She has seen her twice in that same stairway since she moved in six months ago. She also thought the shadow she saw on the walls occasionally was just that, but realized it was a ghost after it appeared in different locations of the house; once manifesting itself in the center of the room.

Dee explained the history of sightings to her neighbor, and assured her that despite scaring the beejeezes out of her, the ghosts have never harmed anyone to her knowledge.

As Dolores related this story to me she asked, "Sis, do you think the ghosts from our house jumped next door?"

"Sounds like it. Keep in mind that the Burton house was blessed, which you would think would send them to be with God. It evidently just sent them about 50 feet away. Also remember that the house your living in was part of a much larger farm a century ago. The house next door was just part of the original estate, as were many houses in the Samuel Bacon allotment. Ghosts go where they want to go. There are no physical restrictions in the afterlife."

Dee said she was going to bring the neighbor a crucifix and some holy water to help her send the unwelcome guests on their way.

Chapter 9

MORE BACON

   Stephen is the youngest in our large family. He and Cathy are twins; remaining close throughout their lives. I don't think they ever talked about what happened to them while they were at Burton. We discuss it often now, especially since I've been writing.
   Stephen is a very successful business executive with a large firm in Cleveland, Ohio. He and his two children live in Akron. They have never experienced any unusual phenomenon in their home. This incident happened when Steve was babysitting at the Burton house:

Subject: Ghost Story

Sue,

My first, only and last hopefully encounter with a spirit/ghost/apparition, whatever you want to call it came in the 3rd floor apartment at Burton when sister Beth lived there. I do not even remember how old I was, but am guessing around 12? I was laying in the living room where she had that burnt orange furniture.
Anyone who ever spent any time in that house, specifically upstairs in the 3rd floor apartment, would easily recognize the creaking noises made by the stairs and the

hallway. The stairs which came up to a landing overlooking the garage, turned and came up another 8-10 stairs to the

hallway where there were bedrooms on either side, and straight back was a dining room, a very small kitchenette, and to the right of the dining room a door that led to the living room, which is where I was.

From the living room you really could only see thru the door into the dining room, but little else.

As I lay on the floor watching TV, alone in the apartment, I believe Beth was downstairs in the middle apartment, I heard the familiar creak of the steps. I assumed Beth was returning. With each step, you could guesstimate approximately which step the person was on as they were ascending to the upstairs apartment. I recognized the lower stairs, as she hit the landing and turned back towards the hallway leading to the dining room.

As I heard the creak of the last could stairs, I said in an almost inquisitive voice, "Beth?"

No reply. As the creaks of the boards in the hallway told me she was on her way, I said again, "Beth?" Still no reply. At this point, I had a weird feeling come over me - not necessarily afraid, but more curious, as though I thought maybe she was messing with me as I knew whoever it was would've heard both calls. As the steps crossed from the hallway into the dining room, I looked away from the TV towards the door. I have not spoken to many of what I saw next. As I looked towards the doorway, I saw a young woman pass by the door on what appeared to be a long white flowing gown. She did not look at me, but continued past my vantage point towards the small kitchenette which measured no more than 5 feet by three feet of actual walking space. Not being certain of what I just witnessed I got up and walked to the doorway, looking to my right.

There was nothing there.

This was the second time Stephen sent me his story. The first one somehow was deleted from my files although his was the only story deleted. Thanks for your patience, Stephen.

He evidently saw the same ghost that had been seen by David, Vincent and my ex-husband. The woman in the white nightgown was the ghost of Bacon's daughter, according to my son Vincent.

My investigation into the history of the original residents of the property has been futile.

In two thousand ten I went to Akron to visit my family and do the research I couldn't do online at my home in Dallas. My sister Dolores agreed to accompany me downtown to research the original inhabitants of where the Burton house now sits. I knew from the legal description that it was the 'Bacon: Lot All'. I also knew that the deed I had was dated 1917, the title was held by the Fairhead family from that date until I purchased the property in 1984. Bacon told Vince the people in town torched his home for Bacon's assisting John Brown with the Underground Railroad, a fire which destroyed the original home killing he and his daughter. There had to be a record of this somewhere in the city files.

Dolores and I researched papers for school innumerable times. The top floor of the Akron Public Library is a research library, not open to the public. We were granted access with my Dallas Press Club ID and the explanation that I was writing a book, so we began our search. For over two hours we poured over everything from disasters in the west part of Akron, to the first phone book published in the area to any individual with the last name of Bacon and decades of microfilm from the Akron Beacon Journal. We found several interesting facts, photos and stories, but nothing relevant to what we needed. I decided to give it one last shot, and went to the plat maps for the area known as Crestland Park Allotment. The security officer must've seen the quizzical look on my face as I examined the page in front of me. He left his desk by the entry door and approached me asking, "Is there something I can help you find?"

I quickly closed the plat book while responding' "Yes, there is. I have been looking for a specific parcel in west Akron with no luck. I know there were people living on the property in the early

twentieth century, I am totally at a loss as to where to find the info on that parcel."

"Well, that should be easy. It'll be right here." Opening the plat map I had just closed as he said this.

He efficiently turned to the last page I was on, and immediately developed the same furrowed brow I had moments prior. My sister Dee joined us at the table in the front of the library where all the plats for the city are located. She was moving her head slowly from side to side; she'd come up empty, too.

"Well," he began, "The parcel you're looking for should be right here."

He was leaning onto the pages, then straightened himself while scratching his head. He bent forward over the book again, this time running his fingers over the page, looking into the seam to see if a page had been removed; possibly torn out. He stood up and simply stated, "I don't what to tell you, ma'am. It's not here. It should be, but it's not."

It was a consolation knowing I was researching the correct location, but disturbing that two hours of our day had been an exercise in futility. I asked him if there was another place in the archives where I could research the area or the house. "Not that I'm aware of." He said.

Dolores was mom's caregiver at the time, and we had to get back to her condominium. As we left the security officer stood, opened the door for us and said, "Good luck with the book!"

Our brothers John and Greg also lived at Burton in the basement apartment for about two years. They were in their twenties and wanted their independence; translated: they wanted to party like rock stars and couldn't do it at mom's house. I liked having my brothers around to help with maintaining an old home, which they did. They both had full-time jobs, but loved spending their weekend evenings at one of the many discotheques in Akron dancing, drinking and meeting girls. Greg met his beautiful wife Stephanie at one.

It was a weekday evening and John decided to go out with some baseball buddies after his game because he didn't have to work until after noon the next day. Wednesday night was ladies night at the disco, so the guys went to drink beer and watch the pretty girls dance, knowing the place would be packed. Greg stayed at the apartment because he had to work early the next day. He had some dinner, watched the top stories on the local news at eleven, and fell asleep on the couch. When he woke up, the screen was nothing but snow, so he knew it was after midnight and was upset that he'd fallen asleep in the living room. He turned the television off and went into the bedroom. He thought he saw something with his peripheral vision move in the kitchen to his right as he stood, but looked into the kitchen and saw nothing there. He shook his head and headed for bed. They'd set up twin beds on either end of the small room at the front of the basement, which was the bedroom. The only light in the apartment was ambient from the neighbor's outside security lighting, but Greg could easily navigate the short distance to his bed.

He was standing in the six foot opening between the living and bedroom; he turned once again to look through the apartment, down the wide center hall into the kitchen before going to bed. His eyes had adjusted to the lack of light, and he saw a dark figure standing at the doorway that leads into the other part of the house. He said, "Damn John, you could've let me know you were home, and what's with that fuckin ugly hat?"

Greg thought it was queer that John didn't respond, but assumed he didn't hear him. He walked through the dark apartment into the kitchen, then witnessed who he thought was John walk out the door into the common area on the basements other side. He also knew it wasn't his brother, but wanted it to make sense in his rational brain. When he arrived in the kitchen, he saw the door to the other side of the basement was locked and chained. Greg stood staring at the chain on the door for a few seconds while he tried to wrap his head around what he'd just seen. He slid the head of chain lock back and forth a few times to make certain it was functioning properly. He turned the deadbolt twice, then opened the door and called into the darkness on the other side of the basement, "John?"

Nothing but silence.

He closed, relocked the door and returned to bed. He knew he'd just seen the ghost his nephew talked about.

John came home about twenty minutes later.

I had my brothers up for beers, food and the Cleveland Indians game the following Sunday afternoon. Greg greeted me with a kiss on the cheek, which he always does and said, "I saw your son's pecker-friend Bacon Wednesday night."

He gave his characteristic chuckle as he said this. Greg is extremely intelligent and witty; the gentleman we lovingly referred to as 'Hoss' after Dan Blocker's character in Gunsmoke. He wasn't frightened of Bacon, just agitated and perplexed. He will always look for a rational, scientific explanation for things that happen; this time he couldn't find one.

He was nonchalant as he told me about what he saw, saying that he thought it was a hat and coat hanging on a hall tree when he first saw it, but realized they didn't have a hall tree next to the door. When it moved, he thought it was his brother, of course. He described the same entity that Lois described to me. What Greg didn't know until months later was that John and others had seen the exact same thing in that part of the basement as well.

John is a baseball player, has been his entire life. He very physically fit, has a quick sense of humor, and an equally quick temper, especially when it comes to protecting those he loves. When I asked John if he would send me an e-mail about his encounters with Bacon, he said "No. I'm a caveman and I don't use computers. I prefer you tell my story." So here goes...

John moved into the basement apartment several months before his brother Greg joined him. He worked full time as a painter and played baseball for three AA clubs at the time. He was engaged to his high school sweetheart, and his life was in constant motion from the time his feet hit the floor early in the morning until after the news at eleven o'clock, Monday through Friday, sometimes on Saturday and Sunday as well.

He was sitting on the couch watching the late news while he ate a pizza, and after the sports broadcast turned off the set. It was an old television, the kind when turned off kept a small whitish-blue dot in the center of the screen which gradually fades to black. He saw something pass by the screen in front of the dot, but knew he was alone and nothing could've passed between him and the television. It happened again and he turned to see what he later realized was Bacon exiting the door going into the other side of the basement.

He saw a dark figure, wearing a hat and what he described to me as "a long coat, more like a western style duster."

John immediately grabbed his bat and headed for the door, intent on using it if necessary. (A bat is a weapon in a baseball player's hands). The door was unlocked but closed. He flung it open and went into the other side of the basement, bat up and ready to swing. It was dark and quiet. He turned around to go back into his place, resting the bat on his shoulder. He looked up the stairs to his right and could see that the door to the garage was locked and chained as well.

He would've heard someone opening or closing doors had a person been there. He was confused when he went to bed.

His fiancée Audrey would usually spend the weekend with him. She was attending college and working full-time, so Saturday and Sunday they often spent together. Saturday after going out they fell asleep around midnight, exhausted. John wasn't certain of what caused him to awaken, nor did he know what time it was, but he woke up to see a figure looming over him on his side of the bed, appearing to reach over him towards Audrey. He tried to yell, but was so terrified that nothing came out of his mouth. He said it felt as though he was being choked, starving for oxygen and adrenaline at the same time. He does remember closing his eyes and thinking, 'Lord, give me strength.' He opened his eyes and the figure was still over him, reaching for Audrey. He swung his fisted left arm toward the dark figure as mightily as he could, so hard in fact that he woke Audrey. The ghost disappeared instantly. She rubbed her eyes and asked groggily, "What are you doing?"

"I must've had a bad dream. Sorry I woke you up, honey."

He believed he had a bad dream. He kept telling himself the entire next day and the day after that that it was just a bad dream. Somewhere deep in his subconscious mind he knew it hadn't been a dream, however. It was the man in the long duster with the strange hat, coming to visit him again.

Life continued on, and John had a plethora of roommates at Burton after Greg moved out.

Our mom had to sell the 'big house' we grew up in on Clemmer avenue, so John moved into her new, smaller home to help her fix it up. Greg lived there as well. Mother was always so generous with her time and talents, and would watch my son Vincent when I would travel out of town for business, which I had to do frequently during the mid-eighties. She asked to speak with me privately after I'd arrived at her house to pick Vince up after a business trip. "Sure mom, what's up?"

She asked, "Do you have time for coffee? I could use a cup."
"Sure honey. I could use a cup myself."

My mother brewed perhaps the best cup of coffee you could ever have, which is one of the reasons her restaurant 'Mary's Coffee Shop' decades before was so successful.

We sat at the kitchen table with the double, wooden-sash windows to my right. Mom, like me, loved being able to see outside and would open the windows anytime the weather in Akron permitted. We sat across from each other, sipping our coffee and enjoying the early evening breeze.

"Honey" she started, "Vince told me that a ghost keeps coming to see him at the house." (referring to the Burton house).

She looked troubled as she told me; mother never liked telling us things that would make us uncomfortable. She knew how anxious I have always been, one time telling me when I was just eleven and running late for school, "If you don't learn to settle down, you're gonna have a heart attack by the time your twelve!"

"Mom, Vince has been telling me about this friend of his for a while now. I spoke to his pediatrician about it, and he seems to think Vince developed an imaginary friend because he's an only child. He said it happens frequently."

"I could understand why he'd think that, but Vince is here with me and his cousins, or in school with classmates most of the time. I thought that usually happens when kids are left alone for extended periods of time."

I was not about argue with the expert on children, she reared eleven superbly.

I took a sip of my coffee and thought about how I would hear

Vince talking to himself every night, always at eleven o'clock. I knew this because I'd hear him during the lengthy commercials that came on before the evening news, which I'd silence until the news anchors came on the screen.

So I asked, "Well mom, do you really think he's talking to a ghost?"

"Could be, honey. This man Bacon that comes to talk to him scares him half to death. He seemed genuinely frightened when he told me, and I can tell the difference."

She winked and nodded as she said this, then turned and got up from the table to warm her coffee. She continued as she poured cream into her cup, " I wouldn't discount it. I just want you to be aware of it, and keep an ear and eye out. If the thing is in Vincent's imagination, it may go away as he gets older."

She smiled at me when she added, "If he doesn't, I'll come up with my Rosary and have Our Blessed Mother escort his butt out!"

We both enjoyed a laugh as we joked about the Mother of God physically kicking this ghost Bacon in the posterior.

Mom always had Holy objects near her in the house. They are a source of comfort and protection, and they certainly comforted her and protected all of us from harm. I also wanted to note that Mary Jane was never one to use vulgar language; we weren't permitted to ever use profanity in the home. She'd often say, "It shows a dismal lack of intelligence. God gave you a great mind. I suggest you use it." This time she'd used it for emphasis and to bring a bit of levity to the conversation. Yes, 'butt' was a curse word to my mother.

We finished the evening with her telling me about some insurance policies she was writing and asking about the classes I'd taught. Vince and I kissed her goodbye and left around seven.

John slept in the upstairs bedroom across from his brother Greg at mom's house. He loved having meals and laundry done for him when mom had the time to do it, which she often did.

One summer evening they all watched the news and the three headed upstairs to bed. John couldn't give me an exact time, but knew he'd been in a sound sleep when something roused him. Bacon was standing between the beds looking directly at him, then turned slightly to his left and extended his arm, reaching for his brother Greg. John felt absolute fury welling inside. He told me, "I just couldn't stop saying, Lord give me strength. I must've said it ten times. I came off that bed like a crazy man and swung as hard as I could, hitting him directly in his face. He immediately disappeared, almost like he shattered apart. I twisted and slammed onto the floor I punched so hard."

He paused briefly, then with an impish grin on his face asked, "Did you know your fist goes right through a ghosts face?"

He never saw Bacon after that night, and we can only speculate as to why he chose to torment John by threatening those John loved so dearly. He also told me that he really couldn't make out a face, but knew this dark figure was looking directly at him, almost "taunting me."

A few months later as John was unloading baseball supplies into the foyer at mom's after a game, he overheard Vince telling his grandmother that the ghost "keeps bothering me. He wakes me up, gramma."

John stood upright and became very still as he listened; he heard his mother's voice next, "Tell grandma, sweetheart, what does this man look like?"

"He has a hat and wears a long coat. He's kinda old and looks mean because he's dark like a shadow, gramma."

John told me during the interview that when he heard Vince describe Bacon "I felt like shit was running down my leg! There is no way Vince has ever heard me talk about what I saw up there." (Burton)

Grandma told Vincent to pray to his guardian angel. She made good on her promise to come to house with her Sacramental Rosary, too. I called a priest from our church and he blessed the house. I didn't tell him why, except that I'd never had it blessed since I owned it, and it could probably use one. Several weeks later Vincent and I moved to Dallas, leaving the ghosts behind.

My sister Mary Jane is an intelligent, compassionate mother of six children and several grandchildren. She's been athletic her entire life, and is constantly on the go for her family, the church where she serves as a Eucharistic Minister, or the school district. She earned her master's degree in Speech pathology and has worked for the Akron Public Schools for over twenty five years. She and her husband Mike have been married for over forty years, living briefly in the Burton house. This is her email explaining what happened to her while she lived there:

Here's my account:

In the summer of 1984 the case of a Columbus serial rapist was being tried in Akron.
Several other assaults had the neighborhood on edge. Such was the environment one warm afternoon when I took a nap. Mike was away on a business trip so my night's sleep had not been as restful, the anxiety-provoking news no doubt to blame.

Mid-afternoon sun streamed through the open window of our studio apartment. Whether   I was asleep for ten minutes or an hour I didn't know when I groggily awoke to a sensation of someone bumping the bed beside me.

In a heavy-lidded, semi-conscious haze, I saw at the bottom side of my bed a silhouette of a tall person neatly outlined against the window background behind it. It wore a 19th century farmer's hat, and the entire image was black. As I attempted to focus, the image shattered into thousands of tiny specks, as charred paper blasts apart in a gust of wind.

Closing my eyes for a millisecond I opened them to sun streaming through the open window of our studio apartment. No sign or discernible sense of anything out of the ordinary. Attributing the specter to a dream, no mention was ever made of it.

Years later, after subsequent renters recounted similar, more terrifying encounters, did my singular experience seem to add to the reports of paranormal activities in the Burton house. While I never experienced any sense of foreboding, I definitely know what I saw.
John's description of the hovering image above his bed, in the same bedroom in which my experience occurred, matched my recollection: black silhouette, shapeless body or cape draped over its shoulders, tall farmer's hat on its head.

For two years we lived in that apartment. At no other time did either of us encounter any similar experiences.

Feel free to edit!

Love you

Was the punch in the face from our brother John the reason this entity fractured into… "thousands of tiny specks"? Perhaps, but I'd be more inclined to believe it was prayer that sent Bacon packing. This was the last time Bacon was seen at the house.

My sister Lisabeth (Beth) followed in our mother's footsteps as a realtor and like her mother has been a sales leader on many occasions. She served as the president of the Multiple Listing Service and Akron area Board of Realtors president. She is smart, sassy and savvy. She has two remarkable children and four grandchildren. She and her husband Ed reside in Fairlawn, very close to Akron.

Beth and her daughter Nikki lived in the Burton house for several years and I never knew anything happened while she lived there. I texted her regarding the book, wanting to have her use her real estate skills to find the deed for Burton.(My copy has come up missing.) I also asked if anything extraordinary ever happened to her or her daughter while she lived there. I was floored when she sent this reply to my text:

The only thing that I ever HAD was a photo I took.... that was a shadow on the wall, it was in the downstairs basement apartment, and it looked like an old man with a hat.
I'd love to be able to find that photo!

I'd love her to find the photo as well! I will add that the shadow wasn't there when she took the photograph; she saw it after she had her roll of film developed.

Interesting that John, Jane, Beth, Vincent, Lois all described an 'old man' even though the figure was shadow-like. Again, it's the perception received from the specter itself.

Joan had an encounter with Bacon in the basement apartment, too. She remembered the incident while we were discussing what happened to our brother's John and Greg, and sisters Jane and Beth.

This is Joan's story:

I know it happened on a Saturday, because I was watching an episode of 'Saturday Night Live' when it occurred. You were out for the night, and I was babysitting Vince, who was probably nine months old at the time.

I was watching television in the living room, and heard what sounded like heavy pots and pans being moved around on the stove in the kitchen. (about 30 feet away, to my right) I thought you had come home without announcing yourself, which kinda pissed me off, but figured I must've dozed off and your coming in is what woke me.

Anyhow, I walked down the hall to the kitchen as I was saying, "Hey sis, how was your night…."

When I got to the kitchen, all I saw was the shadow of a large man in a long coat wearing a hat; it was against the far wall behind the table, but in front of it at the same time. I don't know how else to describe it. I stared at it for maybe two seconds, then dropped my head and rubbed my eyes.

I just woke up, I thought. I'm still friggin dreaming.

I opened my eyes and turned the lights on, but the shadow was still there, although the sound stopped.

Then it disappeared into thin air. I flipped the light switch off, then on again. There was no shadow with or without the light in the house, so I knew it was a ghost. It scared me because it was a dark entity.

Years later, as my mom was telling me about what was happening to my nephew Vince at the house, I remembered this incident.

Love you!

Joanie

On the following is a map of Summit County, Ohio from the National Archives, dated 1856. All of the land owners are listed on the map itself, with the exception of Samuel Bacon, who was listed
as the original owner of this parcel on my deed. There is no name on the parcel of land where the house now sits, and where the house has stood since 1917. I've researched the Ohio Historical Society, the Erie Canal Historical Society, the Summit County Historical Society and spent days in research libraries trying to find this man named Samuel Bacon. He is as elusive as his ghost.

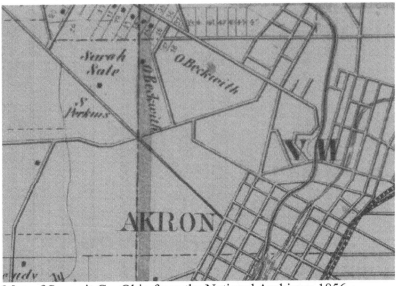

Map of Summit Co. Ohio from the National Archives: 1856

Top photograph has been enlarged to show detail. There is no name listed for the area where the Burton house is located.

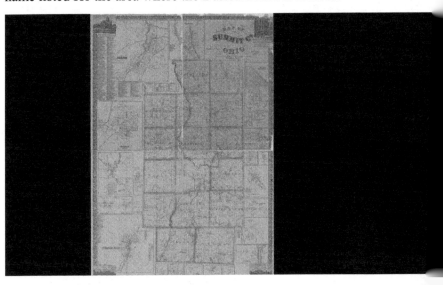

Abstract Title for the Burton property:

> Situated in the City of Akron, County of Summit and State of Ohio;
> And known as being all of Lot No. 2 of an Allotment made by Samuel Bacon,
> and known as Crestland Park Allotment, being a part of Lot No. 11, W.P.P. as
> surveyed and numbered by J.A. Gehres, County Surveyor, and recorded in
> Summit County Records, Plat Book 11, Page 1, subject to conditions,
> obligations and restrictions which run with the land and are now a matter of
> record.
>
> PPN: 67-27834   RTG: 01-01369-06-014.000

This is an abstract title, which simply is a diluted version of the longer, full title. The house is situated on the Summit County map which has no owner's name, but the title clearly states it was part of the 'Allotment made by Samuel Bacon.'

How a five year old would know about the Underground Railroad and tell me this ghost told him of these accounts is unbelievable. Vincent told me I wouldn't find a deed between 1856 and 1917 as well. The map is dated 1856 with no owner listed. The first documentation I found for Burton was dated 1917. Bacon evidently wanted Vincent to know that he was assisting John Brown in the Underground Railroad, an anti-slavery effort to free slaves in the south.

I've not been able to find any information as to who the men were that accompanied John Brown to Harper's Ferry, Virginia (Now West Virginia) in 1859. Historical accounts put the number between 17 and 21 men, but none of the documents I've researched lists their names. I do know that John Brown was hanged for treason and died on Vincent's birthday in 1859.

We may never know, but this man Bacon chose to tell my son of a part of Akron's history that's been undocumented in history books.

Chapter 10

EXERCISING EXORCISM

A dear friend of mine is a Catholic priest who was asked years ago by the bishop of Dallas to be an exorcist. He's asked to remain anonymous. The prospect of facing down Satan himself terrified this priest, and he declined the bishop's request.

He was concerned about my safety while writing about these events, and made me promise to stay close to the Sacraments for protection, which I have. He also recommended a book on exorcisms that is used by priests around the world to study the matter of evil spirits. Along with several others books I read on the subject, I read the book Father recommended and didn't sleep for days; true stories of exorcism are terrifying!

The rite of exorcism has been exaggerated to a great degree by television and movies. An experienced exorcist can tell if someone is under the influence of an evil spirit or suffering from some type of insanity.

What I found interesting was that one of the exorcists I spoke with, also a Catholic priest, never experienced a place that was infested with spirits. He did encounter squeaks, thumps and other peculiar sounds occasionally. His only concern when called to exorcise a person overtaken by an evil spirit is their soul. He often had the feeling he was being watched, stared at actually; I would imagine so if you're calling demons out for battle!

People often told me they felt like they were being watched. I've experienced that same sensation a multitude of times as I wrote this book.

Priests have been physically assaulted while performing exorcisms, one I read about dying from the beating he sustained while performing the rite. Yes, fear plays a significant role in determining whether what one is experiencing is reality or not, but he did not beat himself to death.

The rite of exorcism, its prayers and practices, have been modified very slightly in two thousand years by the Catholic Church. They implement the same prayers on individuals and dwellings by addressing it differently, of course. Usually placing a Sacramental in the place or a blessing is all that's needed to rid a house of unwanted ethereal visitors, as was the case on Burton. I've also read that celebrating a Catholic Mass in the home is an effective way to eradicate spirits.

Sacramentals are objects that have been blessed; most common are Rosaries and Crucifixes. A cross is different from a crucifix because the cross doesn't have the corpus (body) on it. Fr. Chima instructed my brother to place a blessed crucifix at every entrance to keep evil from entering a building; the same was done years later at my mother's condominium. Everyone in our family affected by ghosts have sacramentals in their homes.

On one occasion while visiting my mother's condo, two of my sisters and I were awakened in the middle of the night to voices. Like the Denver ghosts, it was a cacophony of voices; difficult to ascertain how many or their gender.

(Two people I've interviewed while writing this book have heard the choir of angels, and told me it was the most gorgeous sound their minds have ever heard.)

What Dee, Joan and I heard at our mother's house that evening was not a choir of angels, we were certain. Mother was asleep on the couch in the living room. The three of us had just settled in after staying up way too late visiting. Dee took mom's queen bed in the master bedroom, Joan and I on twin beds in the guest bedroom across the hall from her. I was about to drift into deep sleep when the sound began. I shot into a sitting position and asked Joan if she heard anything when I realized she was on her way out of the room already. "Hell yeah, I'm outta here!"

We met Dee in the hall as she was swiftly exiting her bedroom, just as rattled as Joan and I. I asked, "You heard it, too?"

She was trying to tie her bathrobe as she said, "Yeah. I'm thinking maybe they followed me from Denver."

"It sure sounds the same, Dee."

Holding onto each other's arms like the Three Stooges, we quietly walked the condo to see if perhaps the voices were outside. All was incredibly still, except for the quiet murmuring of those indiscernible voices and our occasional stifled laughter from running into each other. The voices we were hearing maintained the same volume, regardless of where we were in the house.

We had to get sleep, so the three of us piled into the queen bed that Dee enjoyed earlier alone. The voices continued for several hours I was told, but because I had the center of the sissy sandwich between Dolores and Joan, I slept like a baby. We never heard the voices again, although Dee had a few minor events happen during the six years that she lived with mom; nothing as sinister as what happened to her in Denver. She felt the floor 'bump' her feet while she did laundry one day, and felt the same thing while doing dishes after dinner one evening. It was very similar to the sensation I had while sweeping Joanie's kitchen.

Dolores and Celia went through the condominium with holy water and prayers to rid the home of spirits after talking to their parish priests. (They attend different Catholic churches.) The condo had to be sold after mom passed in 2012.

Our sister Beth was videotaping the condo for another realtor, as the selling agent couldn't be there for the final walk-through. As Beth worked her way through the place taking video, her two-year-old granddaughter ran into the corner where her great-grandmother sat every day in her recliner, and began rocking back and forth singing, as though her great-grandmother was rocking her, singing her a lullaby. The toddler was too young to have remembered her grandmother doing that. We all believe mom was there with her great-granddaughter, singing her a lullaby that only the child could hear.

Objects that move on their own, even with dead or no batteries, footsteps on stairs and hallways, doors or windows that open or shut, objects that move and are found in the unlikeliest places, animal or human cries; these are the most common phenomena encountered by the exorcists' I've read about, and by the majority of people I interviewed.

Animals are interesting around spirits, too; Celia's cat hissed and ran off just before Celia was hit. My Chow-chow, Lexi, sat staring at a point in the living room days after we moved into our current house. Chows as a breed seldom bark. She barked once, then sat on high alert, staring at the same spot for almost fifteen minutes. What I found extremely peculiar was that my autistic son Paul sat next to her, with his arm around Lexi's neck. He was staring at the same spot, raised his hand slowly as if waving and very quietly said, "Hi."(He really holds the long i sound).

Animals either fixate on a certain spot, or run away in terror. I think Lexi held her ground because she was Paul's protector. Chow's were bred for centuries to guard the Chinese Imperial palace, this makes them incredibly territorial and protective. Our dog did this several times in various rooms, until I blessed the house with Holy Water.

I was looking around my house for the decanter I use for Holy water, because after the second incident with Paul and Lexi, I felt as though our new house needed a blessing. My daughter Genevie happened to be in the children's bathroom so I asked her, "Honey, do you know where my holy water is?"

"It's gone. I washed my eyes with it after I saw a ghost."

I was flabbergasted! My immediate thought was, not again!

She began to cry. I walked to her and put my arms around her, holding her close. "Sweetheart, tell me what happened." I wiped tears from her cheeks.

"I was standing here, in front of the mirror brushing my teeth, and a white light came out of the mirror. It had a bunch of different bright lights in it and all around it." She was contorting her hands and arms in a twisting motion as she spoke, trying to duplicate the motion it made.

"It came out here, and went all the way over here…"

She said as she took my arm and led me into the hallway, stopping in front of a picture of the Sacred Heart of Jesus my aunt Dolores had blessed and given to me as a wedding gift. Genevie pointed at the picture on the wall. "Then it went in there."

"*What* went in there, honey?"

"The light from the mirror, mom!"

We both stood for a minute staring into the painted eyes of Christ. I didn't say anything to her, except that the holy water would protect her through the night. I simply gave her a hug and a kiss and tucked her into bed. Seven-year-olds have enough anxiety, I wanted her to sleep peacefully.

The following day I found Gen's twin sister alone in the bedroom they shared, studying. I asked her if she'd ever seen anything out of the ordinary since we'd moved in. "No, but Gen told me what she saw."

She answered without looking up from her book. "Oh really, what did she see?"

I didn't want to plant an idea.

"She saw lights in the bathroom."

Elizabeth was very matter-of-fact about the whole thing. I said, "Ya know, I'm thinking it was probably a light from the neighbor's car coming out of the driveway."

I crossed the room and pulled the curtains back to give her a view across the street. "See how high their drive is? That's probably what it was."

I turned to exit their bedroom and leave her to her reading. She put her book down on the bed and in one swift motion rolled off her bed into a standing position by the door and said, "Follow me."

I followed her into the bathroom and we faced the mirror. Liz jumped just high enough to touch a spot on the mirror slightly left of the sink basin, about six inches above her eye level. "Except it came from here."

She put her hands back down to her side and walked swiftly past me, out of the bathroom. Liz was incensed that I doubted her sister. I stared at that spot for a minute, then walked out of the bathroom and slightly to my right across the hall, stopping at the threshold of her bedroom. She was again sitting cross-legged in the middle of her bed, reading. I looked at the position of the window, and walked back to the mirror in the bathroom. Light can't travel around corners. I went into her bedroom and kissed her on her forehead. "I believe her. Say your prayers before you go to sleep."

I attended morning Mass the following day and stopped on my

way out to refill my Avon decanter that doubled as a holy water bottle. As luck would have it, the priest and I were exiting the church at the same time so I asked him, "Father, can you come over and bless my new house?"

He was walking at an incredibly fast pace towards the rectory, I knew he was extremely busy. "You're good friends with the deacon, aren't you? I've asked the deacons to help me with that sort of stuff. Give him a call."

It was difficult for me to keep step with him. "Normally I would, but my daughter saw a ghost."

He stopped so abruptly that I ran into him. I apologized as he spun around to face me directly, "Really? Did she see a poltergeist or ghost?"

"She said she saw a ghost, I don't know the difference."

His demeanor changed altogether. I quickly explained to him what she saw. "How old is she again?"

"Seven."

"Oh, then she'll be ok."

He started walking in the direction of the rectory again, although not as quickly. "Father, what do you mean by, she'll be ok?"

"Your kids have been baptized. Ghosts can scare them, but they can't harm one already claimed by Christ. Not a child."

He stopped and faced me again." I'd love to come bless your new house, but I have to get to the hospital this morning to administer the sacrament of the sick to three parishioners. I have a funeral Mass at two and a wedding at four..."

I raised my hand to stop him. "I know you're insanely busy. I got the holy water. I can do this."

I raised my decanter to show a full eight ounces. As he turned once again he laughingly said, "Do you believe some people use it as bath water to spiritually cleanse themselves?"

I smiled, thinking about Gen washing her eyes with it as I made my way to the car.

He and I spoke frequently after I began to write, and I've kept my promise to him to stay close to the sacraments.

Later that night at work in the salon I tried discreetly to tell my friend as I cut her hair what happened with Gen. There was only one other hairdresser working as late as myself, and her station was directly behind mine. Her client overheard me talking and approached us as I worked. "I'm sorry, I didn't mean to eavesdrop, but I heard you talking about what your daughter saw and I've seen the same thing."

She was talking in a brisk but hushed tone, as though she was worried someone would overhear her in an otherwise empty salon. "I was in a car accident two years ago. The paramedics thought I was dead at the scene, I thought I was too. I remember the other car coming towards me, then all I remember seeing were the white lights, almost like bubbles but extremely bright, but not enough to hurt my eyes. They floated and went through my front windshield. I sensed that they wanted me to follow them. I believe they were angels. I woke up two days later in the hospital, and was there almost a month recovering from my injuries. The doctors told me it was a miracle that I was alive."

Because what Gen saw were extremely bright and went into the painting of the Sacred Heart, I believe my daughter saw angels as well. Something evil wouldn't attempt to go near a Sacramental; quite the opposite, evil is repulsed by anything Godly.

Another event happened while I was at work in July of 2006. It was my first day back at work after being in Akron for a week to attend my father's funeral Mass. I started at four o'clock that Friday afternoon. My client was due for color, and I began my application shortly after she arrived. As I applied color to her grey roots, we chatted about my trip and family, and I asked about what she'd been doing since I saw her last. I chastised her for cutting her lawn that morning; it was entirely too much for a sixty-three year old woman to be doing, especially with the heat index in Dallas being over one hundred degrees that morning. She enjoyed the exercise, she said, but it was more difficult that morning, probably because of the heat, she reasoned. I had to do a haircut on another client while Sharon's color processed for thirty minutes, so I got her a glass of water, and had her sit in the pedicure chairs, which are in a private area of the salon. I shut the lights so she could rest quietly, told her to relax and left to do

my haircut.

I was finishing Kathie when another stylist, Deedra, approached me and said, "Sharon isn't looking so good. I got her another glass of water and some crackers, but maybe she should see a doctor."

"Thanks, Dee. I'm ready to get back to her now." I said.

I finished my business with Kathie and immediately went to the center of the salon to retrieve Sharon. Deedra was right, she didn't look like she felt well, the pallor of her skin had me concerned. "Sharon, how bout I get that color off your hair and just style it today? You'll be ok without a haircut for another week."

Sharon was a weekly client and had been with me for over ten years; I considered her more like extended family.

"I think that would be a good idea. I don't feel well."

We walked to the shampoo bowl and I turned the water on to test the temperature as she made herself comfortable reclining in the chair. I thought about asking her if she'd go to the doctor right after her appointment, but thought it best to wait until after the shampoo. I began by rinsing the front center of her head at the hairline, letting the warm water cascade down her scalp until it ran clear. She had her eyes closed and looked very relaxed, but I sensed something was wrong.

"Sharon?" I asked very softly. Her eyes opened, but before she could speak her pupils dilated to the size of her complete iris. I was looking into black eyes instead of her beautiful hazel ones.

I shut the water off and yelled "911!" to no one in particular. Knowing from experience what was coming next, I put my right arm under her shoulders, lifting her upper body out of the chair and rigidity happened almost simultaneously. Adrenaline must've taken over, because as I held her with my right arm I reached under her stiffened body and grabbed the arm of the shampoo chair with my left hand, throwing it perhaps two feet away from us so I could get her onto the floor without hurting her. The entire time I was saying, "Hold on, girlfriend, I got you", and kept repeating, "It's gonna be ok, it's gonna be ok."

I believe now that I was talking more to myself. I looked up briefly to see another co-worker, Kelly, staring at me in disbelief. I yelled 911 again, and she immediately flipped open her cell phone. A gentleman had walked in and was standing at the front desk, she later told me she looked at him and hung up her cell phone, calling paramedics instead on the hard line, so they'd automatically have the address.

I was still trying to get Sharon onto the floor without letting her fall onto the tile, causing further injury, when the young man from the front desk came over to help me. We got her on the floor with towels under her head, and I started CPR. Another client, who was a nurse, came to assist me. The young man opened the door for the paramedics when they arrived. They had to shock her twice, but got a pulse, and transported her immediately. The young man held the door for them as they exited.

As you can imagine, I was in a slight state of shock, as was the entire salon. Several of the other hairdressers and I worked for almost fifteen years together, and had helped each other through some very strenuous times in our lives. This was the first time we'd had a cardiac arrest in the salon, and several of them commented on how quick I was to act. After hours most of us stayed to discuss what happened. Deedra said, "I hope you're working if anything ever happens to me, I wouldn't have known what to do, except probably stand there and scream."

We all laughed. I said, "When I was performing CPR I felt someone rubbing my neck."

Betty laughed and said, "I didn't know what the heck to do, so I figured I'd give you a neck massage while you worked on her."

How can you not love Betty Sue?

I asked the small group, "Does anyone know who that guy was that helped me put her on the floor? I'd like to thank him."

Kelly was the first to answer as the others shook their heads no. "I looked at him right after you yelled 911 the second time, which I really thought at first you were joking about. It was like he told me telepathically to use the hard line instead of my cell phone so the paramedics would have the address from the call. I never thought of that on my own."

"Kelly, there are two things I never joke about, and one of them is 911."

I'm known as a practical joker at work. She asked, "What's the other?"

"I'll let you know as soon as it happens."

I looked around at their faces, "Does anyone know this guy?" I asked the group.

Again, blank stares. Then Darlene added, "I never saw him walk in."

Her work station was next to the window, she saw everyone as they arrived at the door facing south. Then she asked, "Did anyone talk to him?"

No one said anything to him, but I found it odd that he never spoke the entire time he was there, either. Not one of us saw him come or go, nor had any of us ever seen him in the salon before, and never saw him again after that day. Although Darlene joked that if he had just walked in for a haircut, he may have had second thoughts after seeing what was going on!

He was in his early thirties; sandy blonde to light brown hair. Average build and height, and had very well-defined arms.

Because I was revisiting body-building and sculpting at the time, I noticed his forearms as he gently laid Sharon on the floor.

He was wearing a white t-shirt and jeans. Aside from that pretty plain looking, neither extremely handsome or bad looking. I remember looking up to see him as I called for help the second time, and him being at Sharon's feet to help me place her gently on the floor.

The last I remember seeing him was holding the door open for the paramedics as they exited with Sharon on a gurney.

Sharon was put in ICU at the closest hospital, and her daughter came up from Austin, Texas immediately after receiving the news. It's a bit over a four hour drive on a good day.

Sharon had been widowed since I met her ten years ago, and only had the one child. Her daughter called me Sunday to tell me that her mother had passed, and asked me to meet her at the salon, which I did. I was so saddened by the loss of my friend. Her daughter wanted to thank me personally for the action I took to save her mother's life. She said the hospital staff told her that my efforts kept her alive long enough for her daughter to arrive to say goodbye, which meant so much to her.

I told her of the strange man who arrived at the shop long enough to assist, and who we collectively believed was Sharon's guardian angel. Her daughter wept softly, and told me that her mother told her years before that she believed her guardian angel was male, because she and her daughter needed a man around to help protect them after her husband died.

There are exorcists in every religion and culture. American Cherokee Indians have a story of two combatant wolves, one evil; filled with envy, jealousy, greed and hatred; pretty much the seven deadly sins. The other wolf is good; filled with kindness, love and compassion; or the seven virtues. The wolves represent our spiritual selves. Who wins the battle between the two combatant wolves?
The one you feed.

All humans fight the same battle spiritually. Dealing in that realm, however, is good versus evil on steroids. Our minds have difficulty with the things that we can't explain with our senses, and this showdown cannot be explained, even though we see it every day. Evil forces, or spirits, are the reason people do horrible things to each other, and every religious denomination prays to a God to overcome the shortcomings of man; we must continue to do so.
We've prayed for all the eternal souls tormented in a state of unrest, and for those who have seen and experienced these phenomena. Still, hauntings go back even further with our family.

Mary Genevieve (Poulain) Genevie and Vincent (VC) Genevie

Chapter 11

BENNETT BURGLAR

My maternal grandparents are Vincent Charles and Mary Genevieve (Poulain) Genevie. (That is why I named my daughter Genevie). They moved to the small town of Weston, West Virginia to rear their children; my grandfather wanted to be a glass blower, not following his father's trade as a butcher, and Weston had two of the most productive glass factories in the United States. My grandfather was often called Chauncey or VC by his friends and family, Mary Genevieve most often referred to as Mary. When Chauncey was close to retirement, they moved from the large family house on Center Street to a duplex on the top row of houses that backed into the side of an Appalachian mountain. It gave a spectacular view of the town beneath it, including the state asylum that Weston became famous for. The asylum was always considered haunted by the locals; a television documentary of the hauntings aired years later verifying their suspicions.

When my grandparents lived in Weston, the hospital was still operating as a mental institution; many people in the small town were employees there. Although my grandmother and her daughter Elizabeth (Betty) were nurses, they never worked at the state hospital, although they had several friends that did. We heard many stories growing up about the residents.

The hospital was closed in 1994 because of a lack of federal funding. Many mental institutions across the country were closed during the same decade, leaving those with mental infirmities to fend for themselves on the streets if they weren't taken in by family. The Weston State Hospital is now privately owned and is on the state's registry of historic places. No one in the family who experienced paranormal activity in the Weston house on Bennett Avenue attributed it to the hospital, but we couldn't rule it out, either.

The house on Bennett was the last row of houses sitting on the side of a mountain. Access to the house by car was best done by taking a right turn onto Bennett after two steep grades on East Second and High St, with the row of houses only on the left of the hill behind you, and flooring your car in reverse up the steep grade of the dead end street. My aunt and Grandparents would park on the opposite side of the street and climb the twenty or so stairs to get to their top floor half of the house. It was tiresome if you are young and fit, which is probably what kept my grandparents in such great shape.

When my brother Dave was about 10 months old, my mother decided to make the four hour plus drive to Weston to visit her parents. Her second child, my sister Dolores, had been born prematurely and would spend the first three months of her life in intensive care. In the early nineteen fifties, parents weren't permitted in the neonatal intensive care unit. Mom needed the rest after Dolores was born, and the support and wisdom of her parents. She would often tell me that the mountains gave her a new perspective on life.

After the long drive and dinner the baby was ready to go to bed. The following is my mother's recollection of the story:

"Mother asked me to put the baby upstairs in the back bedroom, and come back downstairs if I felt up to it so we could visit longer." She once told me the visits with her mom were always too short.

She continued, "So I was walking up the stairs with David in my arms. He was quite relaxed and just about to sleep. When we were about three steps from the top of the hallway landing, he began to wiggle, then writhe, and eventually started screaming, clutching me as though he were terrified! Of course Mother insisted it was because he didn't want to sleep alone in a strange place. I reasoned that at ten months he's much too young to be aware that he'd be alone. He was fine until I started up those stairs."

So she came downstairs with her baby son in her arms. He quieted almost immediately as she made her way down the stairs and into the living room. She gently laid him on the couch and checked his diaper pins, thinking perhaps one had popped and poked him; his pins were fine and his diaper was dry. She tried again twice to put him to bed in the back bedroom, and every time she tried she was met with the same reaction from her baby.

In reading about encounters with ghosts, I've noted several authorities on the matter believe children and animals are particularly affected by them, especially if they are negative energies.

Mom finally went to bed with David nestled close. She was on the daybed in the sitting room, which is on the first floor.
She said, "I tried several times to put him to bed in the back bedroom upstairs. Every time I tried I got the same results, even when I laid in bed with him up there."
When I asked Dave about his memory of the Bennett house he said, "It was the coolest house in the neatest location. I always felt weird in the upstairs back bedroom, though."
All but a few of my cousins would reveal that same feeling about the back bedroom at Bennett. It was a sensation of torment more than outright fear; an unnerving anxiety.
My cousin Janet sent an email describing an incident that happened to she and her sister while visiting gramma and grampa, as we lovingly referred to them:

On Wednesday, November 16, 2016 7:49 PM, Janet <j.net> wrote:

Hello my dear cousin,

My recollection of events are: On one occasion, I think I was about 6 or 7 Debbie was in the downstairs bathroom and I had to go real bad (otherwise I would have waited because I hated going upstairs by myself) so I started running through the living room and mom asked me to stop running. I went up the stairs yelling back at her I had to PEE bad. I got about halfway up the stairs when I clearly heard someone from the bedroom run into the bathroom and the door slammed shut. I yelled I said I had to pee, get out of there. No one answered. I pounded on the door; but no one said anything, so I decided to open the door. When I did, NO ONE WAS THERE! I did not stop to pee, just ran back downstairs into the bathroom to tell Debbie what happened.

On another occasion we were playing hide and seek. And I went into the back room and heard someone slam the side door (one leading to the front of the house) and also heard someone running down the stairs and along the sidewalk. When I looked out the door, NO ONE WAS THERE!!
There a few others but not as dramatic, once we were upstairs in the back bedroom laying around talking (still young, probably 6-9), when we felt a cold wind blow over us; but no windows were open.

Another time we heard pounding on the wall in the closet off the area where Grandpa use to sleep, when went to check, there wasn't anyone in there either and of course the pounding stopped.
I hope these stories help you out and I look forward to reading about the many stories each of us have shared.

Love you sweetie,

   always, Janet

The majority of activity in the Bennet house happened around the stairwell and in the back bedroom. It seemed as though young children were affected more than adults, as was the case with Dave, Janet and several others when they were very young. It may have been a visit from one our deceased uncles, who died very young. We'll all find out eventually.
My grandmother told me a story of my three uncles that passed when they were children. What happened between she and her oldest son, Vincent, will remain with me forever. It's also

confirmed my belief that God has a Divine purpose for us all.

Grandma sat with me on the veranda of my childhood home on Clemmer Avenue in Akron, Ohio. It was one of far too few visits from her. While we enjoyed our after dinner coffee I asked, "How did you ever heal from the loss of a child?"

I knew I had an uncle Richard who died when he was two. His photograph hung on the wall of the back bedroom of the Bennett house. It was cropped from a larger picture of her six children, my five year old mother sitting next to Richard in the photo. My grandmother's soft, gentle eyes locked on an unseen point up the street. "Which one?" She responded, then slowly sipped her coffee while keeping her fixed gaze.

I was stunned and felt immediate gut-wrenching compassion for her. We sat for a minute or more in silence.

"How many died?" I asked just above a whisper.

"Three." She said.

She looked at me with her soft brown eyes, and asked, "You've seen pictures of Richard, right?"

I nodded affirmatively without speaking. As she continued, a slight smile appeared on her lips and eyes. The memories of her children brought her such happiness. "He and my oldest, Vincent, died from diabetes. Richard was two. Your mother was five and remembers him. She was a wonderful big sister to him...she loved her little brother so! They played together every day. Vincent was four when he told me he was going to die. Francis was my second-born. He was the first that died when he was nine months old. The doctor had been to the house to see him earlier in the evening. I'd worked with this doctor before, and he knew the family. He was so good to us to make a house call so late in the day. Anyway, turned out Francis had pneumonia, and we were told to keep him warm and dry. I stayed up all night rocking and singing to him, but he never made it to morning."

She leaned back in her chair and breathed deeply, as though she were trying to find oxygen. There were a multitude of thoughts running through my head. The heartbreak I felt as a mother was almost unbearable. I asked, "How did you get through it?"

"With God's grace." She answered softly.

She dropped her head, and rubbed her fingers together gently, as if praying an invisible Rosary. I put my hand on hers and said I was so sorry for her loss. She looked at me, saying nothing. She smiled with her eyes.

"You said Vincent told you he was going to die?" I picked up on that softly spoken comment.

She winked at me and said "Yes."

I waited until she was ready, then she continued, "Vincent came downstairs into the kitchen one morning as I was making breakfast. He was four. We knew he had diabetes, which in those days was a death sentence. Your grandfather and I prayed that one day doctors would find a cure. Thank God they did after Dolores was born and we were able to save her. Well anyway, he told me that an angel had come to see him in his dreams. I really didn't think anything of it because I always told my children to talk to their Guardian Angels before they go to sleep, but then Vincent told me," 'The angel told me that I was going to be with Jesus soon, and for you not to be afraid.'"

She fell quiet for a moment, then continued, "I turned from the sink, walked over to the table and put my son on my lap. I held him and kissed his face, smelling his hair…holding him tight. I knew he would be with God soon, but I wasn't ready to let go. He died that night in his sleep."

Tears moved like warm molasses down my cheeks. I understood how her sadness could be overtaken by happiness, knowing the one you love is in heaven. What a bitter pill to have to swallow, though.

That was the only time I ever spoke to my grandmother about her children who had died.

There were no photos of either Francis or Vincent in the house because cameras were extremely expensive and rare in the early 20'th century. Families could hire a photographer, which is how the photo of Richard and the other children came to be.

She and VC had ten children, with seven living to adulthood.

This story was sent to me by my dear cousin Cathy, she and

Janet are sisters. Their father, John Genevie, was the sixth born
to my grandparents. He was the sibling born just prior to my
mother, and they remained very close throughout their lives.
John died unexpectedly from a heart attack in July 1983, just one
year after our family reunion in St. Petersburg, Florida. This is

Cathy's story:

Dear Sue,

  I just wanted to write to you about the time I saw Dad after he
died. I'll let you decide if it is what
you are looking for your book.

The funeral was tough because I was not feeling the reality of dad's
death at all. I just sort of made
myself think it was just another family gathering. Plus, I (wrongly)
thought that Mom didn't need to
see us upset because she was so overwhelmed by his death. So,
except when I first walked
through the door and when I was leaving, I barely shed a tear. And
I went home after the funeral to
an empty house.

I couldn't sleep that night at all, I kept getting up and trying to
read, then couldn't concentrate and
would come back to bed. This happened at least 3 times in the
night. I had come back to bed for
about the third time, unable to read, unable to sleep, hardly able to
think. There was a light on in
the hall, but no light in my bedroom and I lay there for a few
minutes and became conscious of a
noise or something coming from the corner of my room and looked
in that direction. I saw a sort
of misty light in the corner, and it started to grow a little bigger and
it looked like it was slowly
moving towards me. I was scared for a minute, but then I felt a
really weird calmness that just
went all over me. This misty light seemed to be right at the foot of
my bed, and as I stared at it, I
realized there was a figure of a man inside. I remember thinking at

first that it was Grandpa, but
the features started getting more and more clear until Dad was
standing right at the foot of my bed. I can't even describe the look
on his face, but he was looking down at me with the most perfect
peace that feeling fear never entered my mind. I saw such love and
peace in his eyes -
sounds almost like a cliché, but I don't know how else to describe it,
though I can still see it in my mind's eye. After a minute (don't
really know how long because I was mesmerized) I realized he
was beginning to fade and felt so disappointed that he was going,
but I absolutely knew he was happy and ok.
 That feeling of calm and peace stayed with me for a long time after
that.
 I don't know why he came to me and not mom, but I have a few
guesses. The biggest one is I don't think she could have handled
it....she would have freaked out and he knew that. Also, me and dad
had had a falling out (long story, but that's a different story) and
didn't talk for almost a year before he died. He called me and
invited me down for his birthday and Father's Day (they fell in
the same week) after nearly a year of not speaking and we both
never mentioned our falling out.
 Things were fine between us, but I had wished we could have
talked about it. He died a week after I went home from seeing him.
I always thought his visit to me after the funeral had something to
do with that, because I really knew we were fine after that and that
so was he. (plus I'm probably the one person in our family who
wouldn't have been deeply disturbed)
 I have other incidents (more poltergeist stuff) from when I was 12-
13 if you want to hear about
them.

Hope all is well with you Sue. Have a great weekend.

lots of love,

Cathy

   When I was growing up, our entire family would visit our
grandparents in West Virginia every few years. On one such
summer visit, the Bennett house was extremely hectic. My
mother and father took all their eleven children to visit our
grandparents. Our uncle Ivan came into town from Dallas, and
mom wanted to spend time with her brother as well. It was a

sultry July evening, and because the house didn't have central air, the windows were open, fans running full speed.

I felt compelled to extract myself from the festivities and find quiet, which I did often as a child. (I still do.) I made my way outside onto the front porch glider, my favorite spot in the world. It was a heavy metal glider with cut-out tulip designs on the backrest. My grandmother painted it white, and made comfortable, beautiful cushions in a floral fabric. I would glide back and forth for hours, never tiring of the view from their front porch, firmly planted on my glider.

The entire city of Weston below, lights dimming the farther out you looked. The sky was amazing, stars twinkled like diamonds on black velvet. They were much more plentiful there than they were in my hometown of Akron; and then bam- a shooting star!

The universe and astronomy have always intrigued me. I was caught up in the astonishment of the moment when I heard the front screen door close.

My uncle Ivan evidently felt the same compulsion for solitude that I felt. He sat down next to me on the glider, and patting my leg said, "Honey, how are you?"

My uncle Ivan was one of the kindest men I've ever known. All of my mother's brothers were good, kind men. But Ivan was different. He was tall and thin, with angular features. He was a veteran of the Korean War, and sustained an injury to his neck as a result of that war. "Flying shrapnel" he once explained to me. The doctors fused his vertebrae, so he had no motion in his neck. It caused him to have to turn his entire upper torso every time he wanted to look right or left. As a very young child, this awkward movement frightened me somewhat.

"I'm fine, just trying to enjoy the solitude." I told him.
He let out a laugh, then leaning into me kissed me on the forehead. He was warm and smelled of Old Spice. "Okay, I can take a hint."

He bent forward as if to stand. Reverse psychology. Nice try, I thought; but it worked again this time.

"Please don't go."

I imagined he wanted the solitude as badly as I did; living alone as he had for so long. He relaxed back onto the glider and put his arm around my shoulder. "You know" he started, "Those stars we see tonight were shining down on the Earth when the dinosaurs were roamin around."

"I know. I have a basic understanding of light years and distance." I replied.

"Of course you do, you're an extremely smart kid!" He said with his quick chuckle.

The truth is, I loved astronomy as a child, and it's carried over into my adult life. "I love to watch...." I didn't finish my sentence when another star shot across the sky.

"My God! Did you see that?" He was as amazed as myself, pushing forward on the glider as though he'd try and grab the next one he saw.

"I did! That's the third one I've seen since I came out about ten minutes ago. Aren't they amazing?"

He no sooner pushed back in his seat when we saw one of the most incredible meteor showers either one of us had ever witnessed. They came in rapid succession, hundreds of shooting meteors racing across the night sky, their golden tails following, and then vanishing instantly. We sat and watched silently, sometimes nudging each other's leg or arm and pointing in the direction of the event, until some of my siblings and cousins ran onto the porch, their squeals interrupting our bliss. That day forever changed the way I felt about my dear uncle, Ivan Paul.

My grandfather developed dementia in his latter life; exacerbated, I believe, by the trauma of losing his wife of almost 54 years. He remained at the Bennett house with his daughter, my aunt Betty after grandma died. He didn't want to leave their home, or the memories there.

The best way to describe Aunt Betty is exuberant, but that would be an understatement. She was always in constant motion, her entire body moving continuously to perform the slightest task. I always thought of her as a medical Columbo.

When there was a medical emergency, however, she was calm and deliberate. She was a brilliant nurse, and what I learned from her helped me as a mother-nurse immensely throughout my life.

One day while she and grandpa were alone at the Bennett house the doorbell rang, which was quite unusual. Betty could see a figure beyond the curtained glass door, and answered it to two men who had been solicited by my grandfather to "tear out the far wall in the back bedroom."

Betty's reaction was her nervous laughter. She fidgeted with the door lock as she explained to the men that her father had dementia, and that they wouldn't be needing any home renovations.

Grandpa overheard her at the door and became inconsolable, shouting as he made his way toward her, "Oy Betty, we gotta get them outta there! We'll only need two caskets, about yay long," extending his arms about three feet apart as he said this.

She blushed partially from embarrassment, partially from anger, then thanked the men, closed the door fast, leaning into it to keep her father from opening it and pleading with the men to return. She spun around and glared at her father. "There are no bodies buried between the walls of this house!"

She was furious with him for calling an excavation company to their home.

Grandpa plopped down in his chair by the front door, hung his head and began moving it from side-to-side. "No, it's my dad. I don't know who's with him, but he must've shrunk because there's two of them in there, about yay long." Again he motioned with his outstretched arms about three feet, but much less enthusiastically.

She sighed as she was moved with pity for him. She sat on the arm of the recliner and began to rub his neck as she spoke in a very gentle voice. "Dad, I know you miss your father. We've been to his graveside many times. He's not here in this house. He never was. You know that."

He looked directly at her, his crystal blue eyes moist and searching and asked, "Then who is?"

After my grandparents left this world, my mother went to West Virginia to help her sister settle the estate and sell the house. Betty decided she'd leave West Virginia and move to Florida to be close to her sister Dolores and brother-in-law, Tom. Dolores was a diabetic from birth, suffering from all the complications that accompany such a devastating disease. Tom was asthmatic, and she wanted to be close to them should they require medical care; they invited her to live with them for the same reason. The family had already lost two siblings to diabetes, they were very protective of their youngest and did what they could to protect her.

Aunt Betty also told me she wouldn't miss the West Virginia winters at all. "I can't wait to get to sunny Florida!" She said.

Mom and her sister poured through the contents of the house, making piles in different rooms as to what to keep, what to trash and what to give away. They were exhausted and emotionally drained as they both ascended the stairs to bed that night. Betty went into her room on the right at the top of the stairs, mom taking her parents room on the left; she made herself comfortable in her parent's bed and enjoyed being in their room, relishing the things they'd touched. She told me she started to pray the Rosary when her quiet was disturbed by the sound of footsteps on the stairs. The third step from the top where the stairs triangularly pivot to the left creaked. Her immediate thought was that someone who'd read her father's obituary had come to the house to vandalize, assuming it was empty. (I know, sad that people could stoop so low.) Her mind swam. She immediately looked around the dark room to find a weapon, and seized the closest thing she could find, her father's cane which was still propped against the headboard.

Trying to remain as quiet as possible, she braced herself between the bed and dresser for firm footing, then brandished the cane high over her head with her left hand and opened the door forcefully and quickly with her right. (She was left handed.) The element of surprise alone might knock him down the stairs, she thought. As she did this she yelled, "What the hell do you want?" No one was there.

She said she felt like someone was standing in front of her, but there was no one.

Aunt Betty appeared in the threshold of her bedroom directly across from her, tying her robe at the waist, the blinder shades she always wore when she slept pushed up on her forehead. "Mary Jane, what is it?"

"I heard someone, Betty. Someone's broken in."

"Oh, that's not possible. This house is like Fort Knox. We made sure all the doors and windows were locked just a bit ago. Now go to bed."

Betty turned to go back into her room, but mom insisted. "Betty, I know what the hell I heard. I'm going downstairs!"

Armed with her father's cane, down she started. Betty came in behind her. "Oh hells-bells Mary, you're dreaming!"

Mary Jane checked the house like a prison watchman, always on alert and cane ready with Betty following, talking constantly about how nonsensical this endeavor was. The place was secured, no signs of entry anywhere. They went back to bed.

A few days passed, the house was becoming more and more open. All of their parent's personal effects had been given away, or boxed with names in the living room for various family members. Their brother, my uncle Lou, came from Levitown, Pennsylvania to assist his sisters any way he could. He brought his son Richard and daughter Kathy, the two youngest of Lou and Isabel's six children.

Richard is quiet, kind and extremely intelligent. He has always been his father's right hand man, taking care of him until his death in December, 2012.

Aunt Betty asked her nephew if he'd mind going through the boxes of paperwork in the closet next to the fireplace. Richard happily obliged and started to work. Save what's important, Aunt Betty told him, "You know, current insurance documents, car titles. You know what's important. If you're unsure, just ask. Pitch the rest."

Betty was off like a tornado to her next task.

Richard settled in front of the doorway to the closet, sitting cross-legged on the floor. He had a trash bag to his right, and a small box on his left for what to keep. It wasn't long before he happened upon a news article dated February 14'th, 1927 from a Rochester, PA. newspaper. 'Frozen Body of Missing Man Found in Quarry' were the headlines.

We'd heard the story of my grandmother's brother Jim Poulain being murdered, his murderer acquitted, but this was the story in its entirety in the closet. Rich couldn't believe it had been there all these years, probably cut from the paper by our grandmother.

The newspaper stories then are not what they are today. It told of Jim's family, '...he leaves a wife and five children...' then gave their ages, 1-11 years old. 'Left home December 26'th with two men to return a sweater he'd purchased for his sister who resides in West Virginia...'

Richard couldn't believe what he was reading!

Jim Poulain left home with his brother-in-law, Mark Hill and another man, a Mr. Irons. They arrived at his home the day after Christmas, 1926, wanting him to accompany them for a drink. Jim's wife reluctantly agreed, since he and Mark had several arguments stemming from their four recent car accidents. She hoped they could mend their relationship over a drink. The three men left the house around 2:00 in the afternoon. Jim took the red sweater he'd purchased for his sister Mary; wanting to exchange it for a white one for her while he was out.

The three had a good time at the local speakeasy until the bartender refused to serve the men alcohol. "He was inebriated when he came in." gesturing towards Mr. Irons as he said this in court.

This was the man my great uncle didn't know well, so when they left the bar and Mark's car broke down, Jim was uneasy about walking the few miles toward home with Irons. Mark lived in the opposite direction and started for home immediately. Jim had no choice, so he started home on foot with the stranger, Mary's sweater tucked under his arm. Irons was cursing the bartender for cutting him off; had been since they left the pub. He was extremely agitated, having once, "Stomped a pig to death because he was angry," A female neighbor of his recounted in court.

That was the last time Jim Poulain was seen alive.

In February as a paperboy was bicycling over the Beaver Creek Bridge, he noticed something out of the corner of his eye in the quarry below. He got off his bike and made his way down the steep embankment to the red object he saw protruding through the melting snow. It was Mary's sweater; Jim still had it in his hands. The boy was horrified to see the hand. He pedaled home as fast as he could, and between gasps told his mother what he'd found. Trembling, she called the sheriff's office, who in turn went immediately to secure the area. The sheriff testified in court, "The body was well preserved because of the snow and freezing temperatures. The extremities had been chewed by animals, but we were able to recognize Jim immediately. He'd been missing from his family for almost two months, and that's not like Jim. Because the body was so well preserved, we could make out the imprint of several shoe marks on his chest."

The shoe imprints found on Jim Poulain's chest were an exact match, both in size and design, to a pair owned by the man who was last with him, Mr. Irons. Later in open court, after Irons was acquitted, the sheriff's deputy that found the body stood and pointing at the accused shouting, "Murder will out!"

No one was ever brought to justice for the murder of Jim Poulain.

Richard was dumbfounded by what he read. He jumped up, papers falling around him like dried leaves as he raced across the house calling for his aunt. He found her on the back porch having a cigarette. "I need this article, Aunt Betty."

He was writing a book about his paternal side of the family and wanted to include the story. "No, you can't have it. I'll keep the original, that was mothers. You can make a copy if you want."

She no sooner got that out of her mouth that Rich was on his way downtown to the copy machines at the five and dime store. The news article wouldn't copy. The name of the paper and date were readable, but the contents of the copy were smeared, like someone had wiped wet ink. He was baffled, but decided since it wouldn't copy, he'd write it out in cursive. He purchased a legal pad and new pen and headed back to Bennett Avenue.

I once read that being unable to copy something is possibly a sign of a demonic presence.

That night he sat at the sturdy wooden table in the laundry room to write. There was one chair in front of the table, and I remember my grandfather cleaning vegetables from my grandmother's garden there. The room was on the back side of the house and secluded from the rest of the structure. Sitting at the table, there was a door to the left of him going to the front, and a door to the right going to the backyard and mountain. There was a window in front of him, and after a few hours of writing he opened the window for a breeze. Deciding to break for a while, he went to the kitchen behind him for a glass of water. He drank at the sink, then refilled the glass and turning, walked through the dining and living rooms to the front door to stretch his legs. The place was dark and still; everyone else had gone to bed. He glanced at the clock on the dining room wall, it was just after midnight. He wanted to continue to write, but his hands were beginning to stiffen. He also knew his aunts would have his work cut out for him later that day. He was only going to be in Weston for 3 days; less than a third of the article had been written. Still, he decided sleep would be best. He went back into the laundry room, closed the window, turned off the lights, and from memory made his way through the kitchen and dining room to the daybed next to the closet he'd been clearing out hours before.

A flash of lightening illuminated the entire room for a millisecond, followed by the rumbling of thunder. He had fond memories of the thunderstorms he experienced in the mountains, and looked forward to a restful night.

Richard was employed at the time as a counselor, working with 'throw away' children, mostly teens, in the Philadelphia and New York City area. It was at a group home; the pay was lousy and benefits non-existent, but he loved helping the boys and got enormous satisfaction from it.

He'd also worked as a lifeguard at Jersey Shore, was an experienced swimmer and loved to windsurf and parasail. He worked briefly as a park ranger, spending nights in the forest alone. Rich is also an avid chess player, tennis player & bike rider; very physically fit and extremely intelligent. He wasn't intimidated easily.

Richard got comfortable on the daybed; he was genuinely tired and quickly felt his mind and body drifting to sleep. It was interrupted almost immediately by the sound of papers rattling. He told me, "It sounded like someone took my legal pad and was shaking it really hard by the binding at the top."

He got up and walked through the dining room and kitchen into the laundry room, hearing the papers rattle the entire time, interrupted briefly by the rumble of thunder. Flipping the light switch on as he entered, the sound stopped instantaneously. Everything was exactly as he left it. He looked to his right and left, then walked to each door to make sure they were securely locked. He checked the window, but distinctly remembers locking it. Everything was exactly as he left it. He scratched his head. He knew he was tired and thought perhaps he'd slept and this was just a dream. He couldn't understand why he'd still hear the papers as he walked, though. Shrugging his shoulders, he turned around, cut the lights, and went back to bed. His head no sooner hit the pillow that the paper rattling started again. This time he bolted up, and turning to put his feet on the floor in front of him, heard footsteps moving toward him from the living room. He said, "I could hear footsteps coming over the cold air return duct on the floor".

He instinctively said as he stood, "Kathy, what are you doing up?"

He told me that even as the words were coming out of his mouth, he knew it wasn't his sister. From the intermittent bursts of lightening, he saw no one in the room, but he *felt* someone there.

He also knew it was a man, but couldn't explain how he knew. The entity stopped just in front of him. He felt chilled, almost nauseated. He said he could feel the cold air on his face as it shrieked at him, *"Leave it alone!"*

Richard stood frozen in place for several minutes, trying to fathom what just occurred. He fell onto the daybed, scared beyond words. He spent the remainder of the night, eyes wide open, trying to wrap his head around what happened, and what it meant.

When Richard told me his story I was flabbergasted. Aunt Betty never gave him the original article, but he had his partial hand written copy which I read when I visited him in Levitown, Pennsylvania with a friend in 1984. He'd given up on the book, and was too scared to pursue our great uncle Jim's murder. He believes it was Uncle Jim wanting to rest in peace. I think it was the perpetrator, wanting to protect his family name and the money associated with it.

Our cousin Ann Marie, Dolores and Tom's only living child, found the original newspaper while clearing Aunt Betty's room after her death.

Original newspaper article about Jim Poulain's murder: Dated February 14, 1927.

My children and I went back to the Weston house on our way to the reunion in Canaan Valley, West Virginia in 2010. The mountain was beginning to reclaim the property. It was sad to see the house vacant, in such a state of disrepair. Wisteria and honeysuckle vines were growing as high as the second floor balcony, but I remembered the old place in its glory, with the bright white metal glider on the barn red floor.

My daughter Genevie stared at the house, her hand held flat and perpendicular to her forehead to shield her eyes from the sun. Her head was cocked to one side, one eye closed, and she said, "Mom, I can see why they left. This place is a mess!"

We all laughed.

We managed to get past the vines and onto the patio on the second floor. I walked its length, and looked out over the Weston skyline again. The city had doubled in size since I was last here as a teenager, and lost that small town feel. My daughter shouted across the patio to me, "Mom, the door's open!"

The front door was ajar, I told them to be still and listen as I gently pushed the door and let it swing open into the house. It was a solid oak door with heavy glass inserts, and it creaked as it slowly opened under its own weight. The tattered curtains blew outward and swirls of dust followed. The paint was chipping on it, the glass murky and cob-webbed. I was somewhat worried that there were people inside. Vagrants and drug addicts often occupy vacant houses.

We were lucky, it was deserted. We all went in, and I told the kids to stay close, which they did. To be on the safe side, I called out, "Is anyone home?"

I held Paul's hand the entire time to keep him close to me. It was the same living room I remembered from my youth, the front picture window with a couch still below it. I wondered why someone would leave a couch. I felt compelled to get upstairs. I was curious to see if Paul would have a reaction in the back bedroom, as I did as a youngster. Crossing the living room, I made my way to the stairs and headed up, the motley, road weary crew following. I was telling my children stories of the house as we made our way up the narrow stairs; I never mentioned the significance of the back room to them, though. The turn at the top was my favorite part; I thought the design of those stairs was so unusual and unique. Then the familiar 'creeak' as I put weight on that third step from the top. I was telling the kids about it as I entered the back bedroom to the right. In it was nothing but a lot of litter; tattered clothes on hangers still in the closet, some strewn on the floor. I walked to the far end of the room a looked out of the murky window into the back yard. The roof of my grandfather's toolshed, about halfway up the yard, was all that was visible through the brush. You could only see forest if you looked straight out because the house was on such a steep grade. Turning from the window, I looked for a while at the darker spot on the otherwise faded wallpaper where my great uncle Richard's photograph hung for years. I felt nothing but my sinuses beginning to tickle. I began to sneeze from all the dust, so we headed downstairs. There was no feeling at all in the back bed room, except sadness for how bad the place looked, and the memories of what it once was.

My son Donald was the first downstairs and bound through the living room, across the cold air return duct on the floor leading into the dining room, and into the kitchen, jumping onto the counter in one fluid motion. "Ah, to be young again!" I called to him with a laugh.

I'd finally relaxed enough to release Paul's hand, allowing him to roam the house. Midway through the dining room, I turned to see the sitting area where the daybed once was. I was thinking of what happened to Richard in this very room when I saw the charred wall to my right. I pivoted, and openly gasped when I saw that the fireplace had been completely destroyed by fire. The mantel and wall, the entire closet and bottom of the stairs were carbon. The remains of what was once solid oak now black, looking more like tissue paper. Those were the same stairs we were just on I thought, as a shudder raced up and down my spine. I can't believe those stairs held our weight! This was the same closet Richard had cleaned out, now a carbon box. I visually continued around the room; the fire had made its way past the closet and underneath the stairs to the side window, on the wall perpendicular to it. It burned through the wall and around two-thirds of the window, exposing the inside of the

house to the elements, and critters! It was as though the window was suspended in air, just making a frame for the beautiful view of the nature outside. I decided to get the kids on the road again. "Let's go!" I shouted, never taking my eyes off the charred wall.
Donald ran in from the kitchen, "Mom, look what I found!"
He extended his hand and in it, a ball of greenish-yellow glass, filled with air bubbles that created a spiral design inside. "Where did you find this?"
I knew it was one my grandfather probably brought home from the glass factory. All the imperfect glass came home with him, and judging from the lop-sidedness of this globe, it was definitely a rejected piece.
"It was on the very top shelf by the kitchen windows. When I jumped on the counter I saw it."
"Then it's yours." I said with a smile.
He held the ball with both hands, admiring his new found treasure. "You're holding a piece of glass probably blown your great-grandfather. How's that feel?"
I asked as I mussed his hair.
"Awesome!"
We laughed as we headed out the door. We made our way to the Suburban, but I had to stop and look at the house one last time. Memories flooded back, and my expression must've given my mood away. Genevie asked, "Mom, do you want to get a picture?'
"I'd like that very much, sweetheart."
We posed briefly, took a photo and hit the road to our Canaan Valley family reunion.

Bennett Avenue: circa 2010. Overgrowth completely obscures view of first floor.

I believe the ghosts that inhabited the Weston house were possibly children who had been buried there. Richard discovered during his research that the house had been moved to its current location, not built on site, so a foundation was never dug. Because of where it's situated on the mountain, the fact that children were uneasy in the back upstairs bedroom, and my grandfather insisted that small wooden caskets needed to be removed from the walls tells me that perhaps a family buried there children there decades, if not centuries prior.

My dear uncle Ivan passed away before our Canaan reunion in 2010. I was in Dallas when I got the call. I flew to his funeral in Abbeyville, SC; coordinating flight times and rental cars with other family members. Ivan's son, my dear cousin Michael, arranged the entire family's accommodations at the famous Belmont Inn in Abbeyville,

I took the last flight out of Spartanburg, South Carolina two days later into a deserted Dallas-Fort Worth airport. I felt vulnerable walking through the parking garage alone at such a late hour, but said a prayer and arrived at my truck unscathed. It was nice being the only vehicle on the narrow airport road south out of the airport. On the brief drive to the toll booth, I reminisced of the past few days and how much I miss my family. Just as I was pulling into the only open toll booth, I saw an enormous fireworks display in the southwest sky. I thought, 'Someone's gonna be in some deep trouble for setting off fireworks so close to the airport.'

The man in the booth stated a price, I took my eyes off the sky just long enough to find and hand him my credit card. Then came another stream of light, this one with an enormous tail and I realized they weren't fireworks at all. I was witnessing a meteor shower!

My eyes filled with tears as I remembered our night on the front glider in Weston, and I thanked God for letting me know He had my uncle in His arms. The man in the toll booth coughed and brought me back to reality; my credit card and receipt in my hand still hanging out the window. Smiling through the tears, I thanked him and continued on my long drive home.

It was that incident that confirmed my belief that there are no coincidences in life.

Chapter 12

TOPSAIL ISLAND

Topsail Island is on the outer banks of North Carolina just northeast of Wilmington.(Pronounced Topsel by the residents there). It was where the Genevie family gathered in 2002 and is one of the most beautiful 1 beaches I've ever been on.

I rented a house on the southern end of the island where there are a cluster of private homes leased for vacationers, so I had siblings and their families as neighbors for the week of our stay. My mother and her sisters, Betty and Dolores, stayed at the hotel close to the center of the island because it required no stairs on the first floor of its two levels. The first floor was even with the parking lot, making easy access for my aunt Dolores who was wheelchair-bound most of the time. A few other family members stayed in the hotel as well: my uncle Ivan, sister Dolores with her children and granddaughter Brianna, and my uncle Lou with his son Richard. (Lou's daughter Kathy passed in December of 2000).

The second night of our reunion, a group of us gathered on the moonlit beach to visit. Our children chased crabs along the sand, wearing glow-sticks as necklaces, ankle and wrist bracelets so they could be easily seen. (Thanks Celia!) I was telling the group about a Cocker Spaniel I'd built on Myrtle Beach several years prior; I thought it would be a cool idea to build a giant octopus on the beach with all my nieces and nephews, or anyone who wanted to join us.

The kids loved the idea, so we decided to build it outside the breezeway of the hotel so mother and those who couldn't come onto the beach could enjoy it as well. We set the time for ten AM, making sure we could get off the beach before noon, so no one would get scorched by the August sun of the Atlantic.

Some arrived with coffee cups in hand the next morning. I got to work piling sand and water into a mound about 3 feet tall. This was to be the 'body' of the octopus. Tentacles followed. I made long furrows in the sand, streaming from the main mound.

Shouting over the roar of the ocean to about fifteen happy kids helping, "How many legs should I put on the octopus?"

"Seven" came the first response.

"Ten" shouted another.

"Why do they call it an OCTOpus?" I really put the emphasis on the first syllable.

"Eight!" Several shouted back in unison, amid screams of laughter.

The beach is the perfect vacation. Kids can't be too loud or break anything. At the end of the day, they're exhausted and sleep like rocks. Parents relax the entire time, just making sure to keep an eye on them.

I finished making the rough form to get them started, then backed off and watched the kids as they began to bring the sand creature to life.

A short stroll down the beach brought me to my cousin Richard, sitting in a chair enjoying the breeze that only salty surf air can provide. He motioned for me to sit, and we chatted as we watched other family members throwing footballs in the surf, playing Bocce ball on the compacted sand, Frisbees sailing and kids swimming. My sister Joan and her husband Vic came by, swinging my son Paul by his arms between them. He would squeal every time his feet hit the water, which made us howl with laughter.

The sculptors up the beach began calling for me, so I excused myself from Rich to check on their progress. I was armed with a video camera, and was videotaping my niece Alaina forming the eyes when someone came up behind me and asked, "Have you seen Paul?"

Not taking my eye from the viewfinder I said, "Yeah, he's down the beach with Vic and Joan."

"No, he's not." It was my sister Joan's voice.

I reeled around and looked her in the eyes. "Then where in the hell is he?"

My sister Dee heard us and came over. I later found out Joan asked Dee if she'd seen him before approaching me.

"I don't know, Sue. He was with us, then took off toward you, so we thought you had him. Now we can't find him."

Joan is known to be a practical joker, so I thought she was kidding. She assured me she wasn't. Once we determined this was possibly a serious situation, we took stock of the family present, and who may have taken him. All were accounted for, except my brother Greg and his wife, Stephanie.

The three of us looked around in every direction, no Paul. Several other family members came forward, and we quickly determined who would look where. I was staying on the beach to search, heading south toward the pier with my daughter Elizabeth and brother John.

Elizabeth began to cry when she realized what was going on and didn't want to be apart from me. I tried to persuade her to stay with her grandmother, who immediately offered watch my three children, but she clutched my hand and began sobbing. I didn't have the patience to argue, so off we went. My brother John is an AA baseball player, having been recruited a few years prior by the Pittsburgh Pirates. He was in terrific physical condition; he needed to be to make the two mile run to the pier. I knew I could make it on adrenaline alone.

My brother Steven and his wife, both collegiate cheerleaders and gymnasts, jogged north in the packed sand close to the edge of the water in their search for him. As soon as Dee left Joan and I on the beach, she went to the motel office and asked the manager, who just happened to be at the desk that day, if she'd seen Paul. After Dolores gave her a brief description of him, the woman said no, she hadn't seen him. She raised the forefinger of her right hand to Dee, picked up the phone receiver with her left hand, called her housekeeping crew and told them there was a child missing. She also put in a call to the police chief. The housekeeping crews were given orders to search all rooms, no exceptions. One room they came upon had a 'Do Not Disturb' sign posted on the door. After a few repetitive knocks, my uncle Ivan appeared at the threshold. They explained what they were there for, and he became irate when they started searching his room, even looking under the bed. "What the hell," he bellowed, "That's my nephew and you're wasting your damn time! He's not here!"

He was outside and halfway to the first floor before housekeeping left his room, making his way down to the breezeway with the rest of the family.

My nephew Mark, Dee's son, ran across the street to a row of houses that were on channels, all of them having boat slips. A boat he described as "bigger than my house" was pulling into dock in its private slip. Mark cupped his hands around his mouth and called to the man on the boat, "Have you seen a little boy, about ten years old?" (Paul was eleven).

"I haven't, what's he look like?"

Mark gave a brief description of Paul, "blondish hair, blue eyes."

The man shouted to his wife who had come onto the back porch to greet him, "Honey, I'll be back soon. We got a boy missin."

He fired the engines and took off for open sea again. Mark told me later, "The gas it took to fire that boat up probably costs more than I make in a week, and he thought nothing of it."

Meanwhile, I continued down the southern end of the beach with brother John and Liz. John would run between houses, checking under pilings to see if Paul had been lured by something shiny or colorful. While he did that, I questioned people on the sand as I went. "Have you seen a young boy, blonde hair?"

Most of the time a head shake from side-to-side was the response. The majority had a sympathetic look, grateful it hadn't happened to them. I became more frantic with each negative reply, trying hard not to show it. We'd made it about halfway to the pier when Elizabeth stopped, grasping her side. "Mom, my side hurts."

Damn! I thought, she's dehydrated. I called to John, who was on a dune bridge talking to one of the residents. He ran to us. "What's up, sis?"

"Liz is dehydrating. I need to get her water." My head felt like it was spinning.

"Get to the showers and get her water."

The residents had shower heads on the elevated wooden boardwalks to their homes to rinse sand and salt. "Those are privately owned, John."

"Do you really think they'll give a damn, considering the circumstances? Go get that girl some water."

He ran his fingers through her hair. "Go get a drink, sweetheart." He kissed me on the cheek. "I'm headed to the pier. You take care of her. Love you, sis." He said as he sprinted away.

I got Liz to the shower, letting the water run until it cooled somewhat. She cupped her hands under the spray of water, managing to get her hands wet, but not much to drink. "Stand under the stream, honey, and just open your mouth." I told her.

She stood under the shower head, mouth opened, and drank. We both drenched ourselves in the lukewarm water. I could've sworn I heard a sizzle as the water cascaded down my back.

We'd been looking for Paul almost an hour. I knew I had to get her out of the sun, which meant stopping my search for Paul. I was tormented beyond belief! I watched from the elevated walkway as my brother ran south, and whispered a prayer of protection for him.

I had to retreat to the hotel for the sake of my daughter. She was dehydrated and sun burnt. We made our way back the water's edge, and just to our right was a woman sitting on a low beach chair in the compacted sand. I must've been so focused on getting Liz to water that I missed her. "I'm sorry to bother you", I started, "I'm looking for my son."

She shook her head no, then quickly stopped herself and said, "He's wearing a white t-shirt with a fish on it, from Cozumel maybe?"

I vigorously nodded yes as she continued," Bright colored swim trunks to match…blond hair, blue eyes?"

I couldn't believe it, she'd seen Paul! "He was behind me. These kids, (she waved her hand to her left) I babysit. These two are mine. (Two children under the age of five appeared at her side).He was making a baby-like sound, which is why I turned to see him. I thought it was one of mine, but was shocked to see a boy his age. He was chasing the sea birds back in this puddle. (Again motioning to her left with her hand) He started to chase the birds into the water, but there was a couple, a man and woman, Paul is his name, right?"

Again, I vigorously nodded affirmatively.

"They said, 'No, no Paul. Don't go in the water,' then extended their hands to him. He ran and took them by the hand, one on either side of him."

"Oh my God, you saw my son! The couple, they were heavy set?"

I knew immediately Greg and Stephanie had him. They hadn't had their three beautiful children yet. Stephanie enjoyed Paul so much, and had spent the night before with him on her lap, playing patty-cake with him. The woman shook her head from side to side. No?

"The woman. She has long blonde hair?" I asked.

Again, a negative head gesture, this time accompanied by a look on her face I can't adequately describe; like she was thinking very hard. She looked up at me from her beach chair, hand in a saluting gesture on her forehead to shield her eyes from the midday sun. "I'm sorry." Was all she said.

Well, Paul was with Greg and Stephanie and safe. It was weird that this woman knew Paul had blue eyes, blonde hair and knew exactly what he was wearing, 'A white shirt with a colorful fish on it...oh...from Cozumel' yet couldn't tell me what color hair the couple had or if they were heavy or thin. They were they only two family members not accounted for at the hotel, so it had to be them.

I thanked her, took Elizabeth by the hand, turned around and headed back to the hotel to get water and shade. I turned back one more time to see how far John had gotten. He was about the size of my thumb, getting closer to the pier. I was thinking of how amazing my family is as I turned north toward the motel ."C'mon Elizabeth, let's get you off the beach."

We weren't 20 feet away when the woman that saw Paul yelled for me. I turned and she stopped quickly to prevent colliding with me. "I've lived on this island for 28 years, and we've never had an abduction."

"Thank you." I said as I grasped her extended hand with both of mine. "I'm sure my brother and sister-in-law have him, though."

I thanked her for taking the time to tell me; we smiled at each other and turned to walk in opposite directions, but I was perplexed as to what made her think it possibly could've been a kidnapping. As we neared the motel breezeway I could see that the patio was full of people. My cousin Ann came running towards us, "You guys, did you find Paul?"

"He'd be with me had I found him, sweetheart. I did meet a lady who saw him with Greg though."

"Thank God." Ann said.

My mother was the first to meet us as we stepped onto the patio and out of the sun. "My God, you're burnt to a crisp!"

I answered with, "Greg and Steph have Paul, it's all good."

There were people on the patio I'd never seen before, mingling with my aunts and uncles who gathered round to hear the news. Mom motioned for me to sit, and I gladly accepted. Elizabeth leaned into my thigh, staying close. Mother handed me a Dixie cup filled with water. I took it but was shaking so violently that a third of the water spilled from the cup all over me. I handed it to Liz, and she drank eagerly. Mom repeated the process, and again with shaking hands I handed the cup to my daughter, all the while relating the story of the woman we met who had seen Paul with Greg. The third time mom handed me the small cup, she held onto it so I couldn't take it from her and said in a very stern voice, "Now you're gonna drink this damn water. Don't you give it to her."

She smiled and kissed Elizabeth on the head. "Honey, your mom needs a drink. I'll get you more in a minute."

She released the cup to me and I cooperated, (out of a very healthy fear of my mother) also because I was feeling the effects of dehydration. I kept telling myself, 'Hold it together. Don't you dare fall out in front of your mother'. I was resisting passing out, taking in another glass of water when aunt Dolores approached. "I can't walk to look for Paul, but I've started a prayer chain."

She twisted her torso to the left with arm outstretched as she spoke, revealing several people who were seated in a circle on the other side of the patio. Some waved to me, others smiled and nodded. "We're praying that Our Blessed Lord will send guardian angels to take Paul somewhere safe until we can find him."

I dismissed her immediately. "That's all fine, well and good Aunt Dee, but right now I need boots on the ground."

I'll never forget the look of hurt she had on her face as she turned from me.

I was wondering why my brother hadn't told anyone where they were taking Paul when my sister Mary Jane walked over. "Sue, the police chief wants to talk with you."

Jane took me by the hand, leading me to the front of the patio close to the parking lot. Halfway across we were intercepted by our cousin Jim. He said to Jane, "I need to talk to Sue for a whole minute."

Then turning to me he said, "You need to sit down."

Jim Genevie, like his father Lou, is a mountain of a man. He's gentle and kind, quick with a smile, usually followed by a hearty laugh. He's also just as pig-headed. At this moment, he wasn't even grinning and I knew something was wrong.

"Dammit Jim, I just stood up. What is it?"

He put his hands on my shoulder and pushed down gently until I was seated on a picnic table bench. "Greg and Stephanie went shopping in Wilmington. They left really early this morning. They don't have Paul."

I could feel the dizziness coming back, as though I was drowning. "Then who does?" I said just above a whisper as my eyes filled with tears.

My sister Jane, who had never left my side, leaned over close to my ear so she could speak softly and took my hand to guide me into a standing position. "That's what he wants to talk to you about, honey."

My sister has her master's degree in speech pathology; working at a convalescent home through college. She had been with Akron public schools for many years, often dealing with those who have mental disabilities. She knew exactly how to handle a crisis situation. Jane and everyone who heard me talking about the lady on the beach knew Paul was not with family. They all also knew that he'd been seen by at least three other witnesses with a man and a woman that no one could describe.

Jane stepped out of my line of vision and I saw the police chief standing in front of his patrol vehicle just beyond the breezeway. We stepped off the patio into the brightness and intense heat of the sun. That's when I saw the ambulance in front of the police chief's SUV. The hotel parking lot was filled with first responders. I looked to my left and saw a helicopter sitting beside the hotel, two men in army fatigues standing in front of it.

As I was looking at the helicopter, Greg pulled into the parking lot. He and Steph were in the convertible they rented, and I could read his lips as he said, "What the hell?"

I looked back at the chief. "What are they doing here?"

He knew I meant the helicopter patrol. "They go up in another 20 minutes. We had officers on jet skis within 10 minutes of getting the call. Air patrol was put on hold because we received news that your son was with family. If that's not the case, I'll release them to circle the island."

Paul has been gone just under two hours. He went on, "Do you have any photos of Paul with you?"

I thought that was a stupid question. Who brings a photo book to the beach? "No, I don't."

I forgot until much later, however, that I had my video camera loaded with video of Paul and all the kids.

"Mrs. Taylor, where are you staying?"

I began to give him my address in Dallas, when my sister interrupted. "She's staying on the southern end of the island..." then gave him my vacation address.

I was staring at her, as though I expected her head to spin. I was acutely aware of the contours of her face, the way her mouth and lips moved when she spoke. "It's obvious to me that my sister is in shock. If you have any other questions, direct them to me."

Ignoring my sister's request, the police chief went on, taking notes the entire time. "Mrs. Taylor, all these houses start looking alike after a while. Do you think your son would recognize the house you're staying in?"

I immediately looked at Jane. Is he intentionally aggravating me? I thought. "My son is autistic. He has no idea that he's even lost..."

I started to digress again, then looked back at Jane. She had become my 'touchstone'. I asked her, "Does he know Paul's autistic? Does he know what autism is?"

The police chief was all business, which I can appreciate. He could've used a course in finesse, however, especially when it concerns talking to parents of missing children. "We had a boy close to your son's age wander off on the beach last week. All the house start to look alike. He was gone over 6 hours, but found severely dehydrated. He's still in intensive care."

I turned my face from him, whispering in my sister's ear, "Is he trying to piss me off? What a horrible thing to say to me right now."

I looked back at the chief and he went on." Mrs.Taylor, we have closed all bridges and waterways to the island. No one is permitted on or off until he's found."

Finally, words I understand and can appreciate! "Thank you, officer."

He turned to speak to his staff.

My brother Greg was in front of me as I turned for the cover of the breezeway. He put his arms around me and held me close, gently rocking back and forth while Steph ran her hand up and down my arm. " We're gonna find him, honey. We just heard and we're so sorry."

I fell to pieces crying in my brother's strong embrace.

He and Jane held my hand as we walked to the picnic table and sat down. Different people approached and gave me an update of progress made in the search. Jim and his wife Judy came over and sat across the table from us. She cracked the pop top off a beer can and put it in front of me. They're like that, they know what you need without having to ask. They told me Richard had gone to the pier (Jim's younger brother). "He told dad he needed the car. Had to go to the pier, couldn't say why, just wanted to get there fast."

My brother Steve and his wife were still running north; most of my immediate family was still looking for Paul. The strangers on the patio were locals who had heard a child had possibly been abducted and came to offer support, prayers and assistance. I remember thinking 'this many people couldn't possibly care.' I was overwhelmed, and in shock. I heard a cacophony of voices, not one distinct unless they were speaking directly at my face. Then suddenly I heard a loud voice yell, "They have him!"

I jumped up from the picnic table and ran in the direction of the voice to the beach. People parted as I made my way through the crowd and onto the sand. John and Richard, who was carrying Paul, raced toward me. I grabbed Paul from Rich's arms, totally wrapping the boy with my body, kissing his face and head, tears of relief streaming down my cheeks. Paul raised his head from my shoulder. "Huh-dah!" He said.

John helped us onto the patio and got a chair for me. I sat and situated Paul on my lap. The chief appeared front and center again, this time flanked by EMT's. Pointing at Paul he said, "We need to get his vitals for our records."

He turned to walk away, then turned toward one of the paramedics saying, "Get hers first. She looks bad."

I didn't care what anyone did or said at that moment. Paul was alive, and not even sunburned! I asked the time, and someone told me it was almost two o'clock. Ten o'clock seemed like a lifetime ago.

Richard never left my side, except briefly to return his father's keys. After the paramedics gave Paul and I a gamut of tests, I thanked them, they packed their bags and left. I was dehydrated, Paul was fine, not even increased body temp. Richard came back to sit with me, John got a beer for the three of us. Rich started in his gentle, metered voice, "I don't know why I wanted to go to the pier. I looked down the beach, and maybe because I've dealt with special needs kids, I just thought Paul would find it interesting. I told my dad I needed the keys. He told me to walk, do you believe it?"

He laughed, then continued, "I went to the pier and wanted to check it to see if Paul was on it. You have to pay to go out on it, so I asked the guy at the ticket counter if he'd seen a little boy. A woman comes up from behind me and says, 'Are you looking for Paul?' then proceeds to describe him! She tells me not to worry, because he's with his parents. Sue, I was freaked out!"

Rich is usually so low key when he talks. He went on, "This guy at the counter tells me he got a call from the police, and waved me to go on. I ran out about ten feet. You could see through the cracks in the wooden slats, and I saw Paul sitting in the sand beneath me. I jumped off the pier and he walked right up to me."

He made the sound Paul makes when he's happy to see someone and we laughed. "There was another kid there, about 13 or so. I asked him if he knew how long Paul had been there. He says, 'as long as me.' Well that was no information, so I asked him if he saw who brought him here and the boy said,' Mister, he's been alone the whole time.' I knew better than to ask him anything else, he'd think I was a weird old man. Well, weirder."

When we finished laughing, John added, "I just thought I was tired after a two mile run in the hottest part of the day. I was about ten yards from the pier when I see this guy grab Paul. I already had Paul in my scope." He motioned as though he were looking through an invisible telescope. "I yelled, put him down you asshole, then I hauled ass toward Paul."

Richard chimed in, "I heard someone yelling down the beach, and realized it was John."

He turned his body to directly face John. "Should I be offended that you called me an asshole?"

We laughed until we were crying. Once Rich regained his breath, he started telling me how weird it was that this woman saw Paul with an indescribable man and woman, but described Paul to a 'T'.

Aunt Dolores came across the patio and was three feet in front of us when I realized she was there. As soon as our eyes met she said, "I told you I was praying that Our Blessed Lord would send guardian angels to take that innocent child somewhere safe until we found him, and that's exactly what He did. God answered our prayers. No one can describe an angel. Why do you even bother praying if you don't believe God answers your prayers?"

I hung my head in shame and apologized. I thanked her for her prayers and hugged her, reminding her that God liked her better than me, which made her laugh. "Oh Sue, you're so funny." She said in her soft southern drawl.

I view prayer differently since that day. I am absolutely convinced that angels took Paul to the pier, and placed him in the safety of the shade until we found him. Dolores was very specific in her request, and God saw it in His will to answer her. It's that simple.

Family members began trickling back to the hotel as word spread that he was found. The crowd on the patio was all but gone as locals headed home. Some stopped to see the boy that created the hubbub on their beautiful, peaceful island and offer kind words. Paul's brother's and sister's arrived after popsicles in their cousin's room and group hugs ensued.

I stayed with my children and several others on the patio until well after dusk, listening to some amazing stories about the genuine spirit and kindness of the family I belong to, and the loving, generous souls that reside on Topsail Island.

Chapter 13

RAINBOW CONNECTION

Being Scotch-Irish on my maternal grandfather's side of the family, my mother grew up hearing stories of rainbows, leprechauns and pots of gold. Chauncey and Mary were both gifted story tellers, and one of my mother's favorite stories was the story of the rainbow.

Sitting on her father's lap one afternoon she asked, "Daddy, is there really a pot of gold at the end of the rainbow?"

He let out a hearty laugh, then bent his head forward to see over the top of his reading glasses, and said to his daughter while looking at his wife, "Of course there is, Mary Jane! Now momma will tell you the story."

He often deferred to his wife for answers when he was lost for an explanation. Mary, sitting across the room at the dinner table continued, "Yes, sweetheart. The pot of gold at the end of the rainbow is your eternal reward in heaven."

The younger Mary Jane cuddled deeper into her father's lap as her mother continued her story.

"Your life is like the rainbow. Sometimes, it's bright yellow and you'll be extremely happy. Other times, it will be dark purple and sad. (She made faces as she spoke). If you stay on the path of the rainbow though, that's God's path for you, you're pot of gold will be your eternal reward in heaven with Jesus forever and ever."

She leaned forward in her chair for emphasis, grinned and winked at her daughter, then continued, "So every time you see a rainbow, you'll know God's let another soul into heaven."

Mother loved her story, and relayed it to us many times in our lives. "Remember to stay on the rainbows path." She'd say.

Every Genevie descendant has heard the story many times, it's discussed at reunions, and passed down to our children and grandchildren.

My grandmother passed away suddenly in 1974. After the

funeral mass at St. Patrick's Church in Weston, the hearse was taking the body from West Virginia to the family burial plot at St. Mary's cemetery in Beaver Falls, Pennsylvania, about a two and a half hour drive. Highway 19 in West Virginia was the route they took, north into Pennsylvania. The scenery is gorgeous any time of year, but especially in autumn, when leaves showcase the brilliance of their foliage. This trip was made in winter; still beautiful, but more in sync with the traveler's mood. Despite the circumstances that brought them together, the siblings tried to make the trip enjoyable; telling tales from each of their different perspectives about their mother and of course, the rainbow story.

As they rounded a curve in the road, there in the sky was one "of the most radiant rainbows I've ever seen." My mother later told me.

They could hardly believe what they were seeing in the middle of February. She had the driver slow so they could all take it in. Everyone agreed that God had sent this as a sign to this bereaved family, it brought them such consolation.

St. Mary's cemetery in Beaver Falls is where the Poulain family is buried. Well, several of them anyway. My mother, her three brothers that died as children: Vincent, Francis and Richard, my grandparents and my grandmother's brother Jim that was murdered, next to his wife and just above their children's gravesites on the hill. My great grandparents are there as well. Their plots are in the oldest section of the cemetery. A concrete angel stands sentinel over their burial grounds from the top of the hill.

My grandfather was never the same after his wife died; he followed her in death two years later. This time, however, my younger sister Lisabeth was able to accompany mom. The funeral director took the same route to the family plot at St. Mary's. As they took the same curve in the road that they'd taken two years before, there were two rainbows over the same mountain pass. They weren't ordinary rainbows. They were perpendicular to each other, forming a cross in the sky.

Everyone who witnessed it was dumb-founded. I've only seen perpendicular rainbows at Niagara Falls, Canada. I understand how the water crystals cause the prisms to appear, but coincidence?

This time, mom had the driver pull over. Many exclaimed they'd never seen two rainbows at the same time, much less running perpendicular to each other. My sister told me, "If I hadn't seen it myself, I'd've thought it was another one of mom's stories to get us to church more."

There are no photographs because no one brought a camera to the funeral. (This was before cell phones, all you millennials). I was never gifted in statistics, but the odds of this natural phenomena happening at the same location, (highly probable) at different times of the year, after both parents passed 2 years apart, at a different hour of the day...It just keeps getting more difficult to believe the rainbows were coincidence. The more I pondered this, the easier it became to believe that God sent this sign. You couldn't take your next breath if He didn't will it, so a pair of rainbows crossing is easy-peasy for God.

Rainbows appeared at every funeral of my mother's siblings, either the day of, or during the service itself.

My mother passed away in April of 2012. Prior to her death she arranged to be buried at the family cemetery in Pennsylvania as well. The funeral lasted several days because arrangements had to be made to coincide the funeral mass in Ohio and the ceremony at the cemetery in the neighboring state. We had viewings at the funeral home Saturday and Sunday evening, a funeral Mass Monday morning, then drove to Pennsylvania the next day for the graveside service. We all drove to the graveside separately with possibly five or six cars in my particular caravan.

My mother was well-known, and equally liked; as intelligent as she was articulate. She was a woman of deep and profound faith, and lived it every day of her life. Family and friends came from across the country to attend her viewings and funeral. I did my mother's hair for the viewing, knowing how much it meant to her that her exterior 'shell' look nice for her friends who would look down on her and comment on how beautiful and peaceful she looked. She just looked dead to me. With the exception of George, co-owner of the funeral home, I was alone with her while I styled the front of her hair. My sister Dolores dropped me off, then picked me up when I finished because I had no car. Dee was mom's primary care-giver, and she had a lot of input into the arrangements. She and George became friends.

Our caravan arrived in Pennsylvania about a half hour before the service was to begin. We mingled with family, talked about travel routes, flight times and family members who couldn't attend. The weather was also discussed, because it was supposed to be snowing that morning: "Possible accumulations of two to three inches..." The weatherman said.

It was sunny with a few scattered clouds, upper forties to mid-fifties by that afternoon. A gorgeous Spring morning in Beaver Valley, Pennsylvania.

A group of us met the hearse as it pulled to the front of the chapel, ten minutes after we'd arrived. The pall bearers unloaded the casket, placing it front and center in the little stone chapel. Chairs were set up facing the casket for the short service to begin. George approached me when everything was ready; "Sue, I can't find your brother Dave and we need to get started. We have to get back to Akron for another funeral this afternoon."

"I understand, George. I know where to find him. Be right back."

I walked out the front doors of the chapel, took a left and another left so I was on the side of the building. Dave was standing midway back, smoking a cigarette. I noticed that he'd look up whenever he wasn't drawing on his smoke, and assumed he was having a conversation with mom or God, or both. Mom's death wasn't easy for Dave to accept, but neither was her sickness when she was alive. He missed the mother he knew, not the one she'd become in the last two years of her life.

I approached him from behind, gently rubbing his back in a circular motion as to not startle him and said, "Dave, George needs to get started."

"Okay." He responded quietly.

He butted his cigarette and looked up. My eyes followed his; what I saw in the sky caused me to run inside the chapel as fast as I could, hands shaking as I pulled the cold, heavy metal handle to the thick oak door; announcing to George and the family that they had to come outside immediately. They all filed out in a steady stream.

Making my way to Dave's side again, he twisted at the waist to see how many people followed me outside and grinned his half smile. We again looked into the cerulean blue sky, the sun shining directly overhead, with a perfectly formed rainbow circling the sun. A cloud in front of the sun looked like an angel trumpeting a horn.

Most stood in wonder and silence, someone ran to their car to retrieve a camera, many had cell phones to capture the image.

My cousin Don, who has been an agnostic for years, leaned over my left shoulder and quietly said, "I believe."

The rainbow is difficult to see beneath the cloud, but it circled the sun. You can still see it faintly at the bottom center of the photograph. The cloud looked very much like a trumpeting angel. This photo was taken by my daughter Elizabeth using her cell phone, perhaps two minutes after she first saw it, as it was beginning to wane.

EPILOGUE

I only thought the paranormal activity had ceased in our family over the past few years, with the exception of a ghost at my home that three people have seen, including myself and one of my dearest friends, Larry Ray Jones. The specter looks like my son Donald, and was last seen about eight months ago; through our steadfast prayer, he'll be on his way to the permanent side soon if he's not gone already.

I believe this family was chosen because of their deep faith and daily life of prayer. As the priest told me, perhaps we did help these lost souls 'find their way' through our prayers. In the sixteen years it's taken me to complete this journey, I've never met another family that's had so many encounters with ghosts. Like my priest friend, I believe the 'family connection' is prayer. 'Family Connections' was the original title of this book.

What began as a day in the life has taken on a life of its own. I began a 'ghost book' that evolved into the realization for me that God truly does control all things, except our free will; our wonderful gift from Him to choose our own path.

Prayers are answered daily; to find the miraculous, we need only to open our eyes and hearts.

I've also learned that every person we meet, even casually, was put here for a purpose by God.

When I volunteered at a nursing home, I befriended a woman who had been pronounced dead weeks before at the hospital. She told me of her experience; meeting people that she didn't give a second thought to in this world; a woman at the Mexican market where she shopped as a young girl, the old post man, immigration officials she met when coming to this country, etc. She said that all these people God placed in her path for a reason. She was angry that the doctors revived her, and couldn't wait to go back to feel the immeasurable love she felt when she passed. (Then she quickly said a prayer for the doctors and hospital staff that she had been angry with). She told me that the love we feel on this Earth is nothingness compared to the love that God and His Mother have for us.

My next venture will be reopening the murder case regarding my great uncle Jim Poulain. My grandmother and her family know the truth now, but for the living descendants and for myself, I'm going to try and bring justice for him in this world, because it's the only one we've got.

The more I discuss my book and faith journey, the more I find friends and acquaintances wanting me to tell their stories as well. I know God will put me where He wants me to be.

At our fiftieth reunion in August of 2017 in Destin, Florida I received startling news. My eldest cousin Lou had been visited by our great uncle, Jim Poulain. Lou has never attended a reunion, and has estranged himself from the family; instead concentrated on his career as a legal consultant. He is incredibly intelligent, with a doctorate in psychology; he assists attorneys in their jury selection.

He explained to his younger brother Richard that he had no idea who the man sitting on his bed was, sobbing uncontrollably; shoulders shuddering with tears streaming down his cheeks as he repeated several times, "It's all my fault! My wife and children left destitute and it's all my fault!"

Lou was moved with pity for this man, and to console him sat up and put his arm around his shoulders softly saying, "It's okay buddy, everything is gonna be okay."

Richard had been busy after his father died going through boxes of his father's memorabilia and photographs when he happened upon a photograph from the early 1900's of a man and woman on their wedding day. Uncle Lou had the photo because his mother, our grandmother Mary, was the maid of honor in her brother Jim's wedding.

When Richard sent the photo to his brother Lou, Lou immediately recognized the man from his dream and called Rich to inquire about it. He explained that the occurrence was so real that it was difficult for him to differentiate whether it was a dream or reality. Lou's wife had the exact same dream the same night.

In a phone conversation Richard asked why I thought the ghost of our great uncle would appear to Lou, especially since Lou hasn't remained close to the family. I believe it's because my dear cousin Lou can help in securing the ninety-year-old court documents from the Pennsylvania courts.

Vincent is grown and rarely speaks about what happened to him as a child. He recently told me that "Ghosts can go where-the-hell-ever they want, and I don't want them near my kids."
He and his beautiful family live in North-Eastern Ohio.

My final words?

Say your prayers.

ACKNOWLEDGEMENTS

I would like to first thank God for my ability to write about, and see that which isn't visible in this world; my family next for their unwavering support, love and contributions to the story; both my siblings and children.

Steve Davis, you prodded when I didn't want to be prodded, but thank you for that and your most precious gift of unconditional love.

I cannot thank enough the technical support I received from Ron Poland, my neighbor and all around great friend; thank you for turning me onto the cloud at 9:00 on a dismal November evening.

Brian Culpepper, my book would still be in PC purgatory if not for you. Thank you for having the patience to retrieve a lost article in cyberspace.

Thank you also to my dear friend, Cindy Croney, for your assistance in researching Samuel Bacon. We didn't find him, but we know he was there!

I'd like to thank Durhl Caussey, former owner of the 'Archer County Advocate' for giving me my first writing break, and his wife, JoAnn Holt Caussey for being a great editor, friend, and promoter. You both believed in me when I didn't believe in myself sometimes.

Thanks to everyone in the Dallas Press Club for your support as well.

Thank you to Gary Jansen, a great writer and Catholic, for taking precious time to read my work and offer guidance. God put you on my rainbow's path for a reason, my friend.

Made in the USA
Lexington, KY
22 November 2017